THE REBEL GIRL'S GUIDE TO MARKETING

Stop Committing Random Acts of Marketing!

Published by
Hybrid Global Publishing
333 E 14th Street
#3C
New York, NY 10003

Manufactured in the United States of America, or in the United
Kingdom when distributed elsewhere.

Raebel, Lisa.
The Rebel Girl's Guide to Marketing
    ISBN: 978-1-957013-52-7
    eBook: 978-1-957013-53-4
    LCCN: 2022917562

Cover design by: Natasha Clawson
Copyediting by: Wendie Pecharsky
Interior design by: Suba Murugan
Author photo by: Miriam Bulcher

www.RebelGirlMarketing.com

Dedication

I dedicate this book to the memory of my mom, Laura Barden. She always believed in me, encouraged me, and never let me doubt myself when I was feeling discouraged. Mom, you will always be my rock and my hero. The beliefs and values you instilled in me will always be my True North.

This book is also dedicated to my husband, Paul, and my children, Alec and Erin★. Without their undying support, love, encouragement, and patience, this book would still be on my laptop and not in your hands. #certifiedbadassmom

I'd also like to thank Pat Miller, Taren Sartler, Krista Morrissey, and Sara Nowacki, who have encouraged, pushed, shoved, uplifted, badgered, inspired, brainstormed, and cheered for me the entire way whilst writing this book. They never let Tina get too far into my head… (you'll have to read the book to find out who Tina is).

Last and definitely not least, to all my fellow members of:

- *Idea Collective, Small Business Incubator*
- *My #GirlBosses Network*
- *And the Wankas… because if I don't mention them, it will be a lifetime of harassment, even more than usual.*

I love you all more than words will ever express and look forward to many more years of laughter, inspiration, and #RebelMindset.

★My extraordinarily talented daughter, Erin, did the interior graphics. #proudmamamoment

Credit for the title of this book goes to Sara Nowacki and Brent Halfwassen

Sara for "The Rebel Girl's Guide to Marketing"

Brent for "Stop Committing Random Acts of Marketing" I LMAO when he said that to me the first time! It still makes me giggle...

Table of Contents

Introduction: Find Your RebelMindset

"Those who stop marketing to save money are like those who stop a clock to save time."

—HENRY FORD

This quote is the essence of why I wrote this book.

Start with a RebelMindset

As human beings, we like to complicate things. Yet if you think about it, marketing in its simplest form is storytelling, and selling in its simplest form is telling that story to others.

You are a business leader, so it's time for you to form a RebelMindset and stop seeing marketing purely as a task. Marketing is a mindset. Everything you do in a day affects your marketing. Yes, EVERYTHING! (I'll explain more about that in Chapter 6.)

Repeat after me: "Marketing is a mindset, marketing is a mindset, marketing is a mindset…" Say this until you knock out any notion that marketing is just a line item on your expense sheet. When you start to look at marketing as a mindset, you will see how much fun you can have telling the world how awesome you really are!

Throughout the book, you will find #RebelMindset statements. These are my way of cutting through the crap and getting down to brass tacks. You will also

I may be showing my age here, yet BRASS TACKS means to discuss or consider the most important details or facts about something

1

find quotes that have inspired me and helped to drive home the lessons taught in each chapter. I hope you enjoy them!

Sound Familiar?

You started your business and take the first customers who are willing to give you money for what you do (at least that is how I started). Then, a few years into your business, you look back and wonder how you got there. You may be working with lackluster customers who are more bother than they are worth, struggling to find talent that "gets it" and working more hours than ever before. There is a saying: "Entrepreneurs are the only people who will quit a 9-to-5 to work 24/7."

I am here to help you understand how great marketing leads to better-qualified prospects, higher profit margins, and less time spent in the office.

Now, I am not saying that everything in this book will apply to you…that would be lying. I am a Rebel, not a fibber. Yet, there are many golden nuggets and ideas that will get your mind racing with ideas as to how to make your marketing yours. It's all about taking what you need out of this book and leaving the rest.

To get the most out of this book, there are two ways to customize what you learn and how it applies to you and your organization. You will find this symbol each time there is a question for you to answer.

1. At the end of each chapter, you will find a place to fill in the questions asked throughout that chapter. Fill in the blanks so you can refer to them as needed while creating strategies and tactics that are specific to what works for your products/services and your target audience.
2. You can find printable PDF worksheets on my website at rebelgirlmarketing.com/guide. Simply print out each chapter's PDF worksheet and fill in the blanks. The PDFs are a great option

if you are reading this book along with your team or mastermind group.

#RebelMindset: Marketing is a team sport! Be sure to share what you write down with your team, mastermind group, or business coach to discover what insights they may have about your answers.

Goal #1: Don't Be a Sucker

Most people have taken a marketing class in high school or college, yet that is where their marketing education ended. You know you need to learn more about this crazy rollercoaster ride called marketing, so you take out your laptop and start searching for a book on marketing. You'll find there are a gazillion books available. (And…thank you for picking up mine!!)

Ok fine. A gazillion is an exaggeration, yet it can feel like that when you are searching for a book that teaches you about the various marketing channels. And I can almost guarantee you that whatever marketing channel book you pick up, whether it is about digital marketing, social media, content writing, web design, or something else, THAT channel of marketing will claim to be the "be-all and end-all" to solving all your marketing and lead-generation problems. It will not.

For example: I was chatting with an entrepreneur who owns a bookkeeping service, and they were telling me about starting a TikTok campaign for their business. In true Rebel form, I asked, "WHY?!?" They told me about an article that said that TikTok is the hottest trend and the best way to gain leads for any business. *What?* I thought. So, I proceeded to ask more questions about how and what they would put in these videos. They had no idea. None. Bookkeeping and TikTok? This is the perfect example of committing random acts of marketing!

> **#RebelMindset:** I am not saying there is no place for bookkeepers on TikTok. All I am saying is that you need to first define your TikTok strategy before you start posting.

Don't be a sucker for the latest trends and articles that claim to solve all your lead-generation problems with one solution. Creating a solid foundational marketing strategy calls for a multipronged approach, starting with building a foundation of understanding the answers the word these five questions:

1. Why do I need marketing in the first place?
2. What do I sell?
3. Whom do I need to talk to?
4. Where do I need to go?
5. What do I want to say?

I know, I know…you already know the answers to these questions. Or do you?

This book is intended to help you understand…

- the direction you want your marketing to take you
- who your ideal customers is and where they hang out
- what problems you can solve for your customers and the emotions that are tied to them
- how to differentiate yourself from the competition
- how to get your team involved in your marketing; there is strength in numbers
- what to say when networking to start great conversations that lead to sales

…and much more!

Goal #2: Don't Be a Statistic

Rebel Girl Marketing's mission is to help businesses stay in business by utilizing great marketing strategies.

Forbes[1] magazine's research found that marketing and sales efforts are among the top four reasons that businesses fail. Throughout this book, we will be working on how to recognize the gaps in your marketing plan and provide strategies to help you fill those gaps.

Small- to medium-sized businesses are the backbone of any community, and we're growing by leaps and bounds! In 2021, business applications grew[2] by an astonishing 40 percent compared to 2019, totaling 5.4 million. Small businesses build stronger neighborhoods. In fact, here in the US, we employ 61.2 million people,[3] which is 46.8 percent of the US workforce!

The statistic that breaks my heart is the percentage of businesses that fail[4]. According to data from the Bureau of Labor Statistics: about 20 percent fail in their first year, and about 50 percent of businesses fail in their fifth year.

The bad news: Yes, it can be tough to stay in business for the long haul. The good news is: You picked up this book! Here, you will build your foundation of what makes great marketing strategies so you can grow your business and not become a statistic.

Strengthen Your RebelMindset by Getting Rid of Roadblocks!

Writing your own marketing content can be hard because it can feel like bragging. I know. Here is my advice: GET OVER IT! It's okay to tell people how freakin' awesome you are!

> **#RebelMindset: It's only bragging if it's not true.**

---

[1] https://www.forbes.com/sites/forbesfinancecouncil/2021/10/08/avoid-these-four-causes-of-small-business-failure/?sh=4b44901a419a.

[2] https://smallbiztrends.com/2022/01/record-number-new-businesses-started-2021.html

[3] https://www.oberlo.com/statistics/number-of-small-business-in-the-us

[4] https://www.lendingtree.com/business/small/failure-rate/

I've been in the sales and marketing game for over 25 years and trying to create my own marketing at times is challenging. I have created marketing content and campaigns for dozens of organizations. I build strategies that show their target audiences they are the best thing since sliced bread. Yet, there are times when I sit down to create my own marketing content and all I hear in my head is crickets.

There are two main roadblocks to creating your own marketing.

1. You simply don't know what to say (we'll get to that in Chapter 5).
2. A roadblock called "limiting beliefs"– you know— that voice in your head that tells you it's not polite to talk about yourself or that you're just not that special. My limiting belief's name is Tina… Tina is a b!tch! (Pardon my French and my apologies to anyone named Tina.) I find it helpful to name my limiting belief so when she starts to tell me things like, "Stop writing this book, nobody will ever read it," I get to tell her to "Shut the &$%# up!" (Here I go again…speaking French.)

Most of the people in my networking groups know who Tina is in my life. When she rears her ugly head and I say something that limits the confidence I have in myself, my friends call me out and say, "That sounds more like Tina than Lisa!" They are usually right.

It reminds me of the Cherokee proverb of the two wolves, it goes something like this:

An old Cherokee is teaching his grandson about life. "There is a terrible fight, and it is between two wolves. One is evil – he is anger, envy, regret, greed, arrogance, self-pity, guilt, resentment, inferiority, lies, false pride, superiority, and ego." He continued, "The other is good – he is joy, peace, love, hope, serenity, humility, kindness, benevolence, empathy, generosity, truth, compassion, and faith. The same fight is going on inside you – and inside every other person, too."

The grandson thought about it for a minute and then asked his grandfather, "Which wolf will win?"

The old Cherokee simply replied, "The one you feed."

What does this have to do with marketing? (Come on...you know this one...) Say it with me: Marketing is a mindset!

When you let doubt and fear feed your thoughts, someone like Tina shows up with her lies and false pride, telling you to stop moving forward. Think of it this way, if you don't believe in yourself, feeding the evil wolf, it's hard to convince someone else to believe in you; hindering your ability to sell and to grow. Yet, when you feed the good wolf, there is no limit to what you can accomplish!

What would you name your limiting belief? Write it here:

_____

Now that we have identified your limiting belief, let's get rid of some common limiting phrases.

Your Assignment: You are going to destroy the next page! This will help you remove these phrases from your mind and all forms of future communication.

You can scribble these phrases out, tear out the page, rip it up, or burn it...whatever you'd like to do to get rid of these phrases—they are not serving you well. You have my permission to be destructive!

Wanna have some fun? Go to the Rebel Girl Marketing Facebook page and share how you destroyed the next page! Once you are there be sure to Like and Follow Rebel Girl Marketing so you can see how others have destroyed their pages! Just be careful not to hurt yourself, or your co-workers, or destroy anything else aside from the page!

To find the Rebel Girl Marketing Facebook page faster, simply use the QR code below:

"The customer is always right."

"That's not my job."

"I'm just a…"

"That is how we've always done it."

"More marketing = more new customers."

> **#RebelMindset: Now that you have removed these limiting mindset phrases, it will bug you when you hear others say them!**

If you still haven't destroyed that page, let's go over why these phrases limit you.

"The customer is always right."

The customer is not always right. There are so many times I have met with prospects who tell me what they need because that is what they read in some marketing article or worse because that is how they have always done it! Yet, as the subject matter expert, it is <u>your job</u> to determine the best solutions to solve your customers' problems. If the customer knew exactly what to do, they wouldn't need you.

"That's not my job."

I work with a lot of small businesses and solo entrepreneurs. I find that the ones who say that marketing is not their job are not my ideal customers. Marketing is everyone's job! Being a brand ambassador, brainstorming new ideas, helping during events, and well, you get the idea…is what makes a great team, and in the end, what makes a company successful.

"I'm just a…"

When people start their sentences with this phrase it drives me crazy. No job or position is any less important than another. Every task and every function contributes to the overall success of an organization. If you don't agree with me, think of what it is like in your world when your workspace is filthy dirty because the maintenance staff did not do their job. How does that affect your mood? How does your mood affect the quality of your work? How does the quality of your work affect your customers? Every job and every person is essential to the company's overall success.

"That is how we've always done it."

If this is what you always say, put down this book because you will hate it. The world has changed. People find and digest information very differently today. Buyers of your product/service are younger, and they don't seek the same results as customers did in the past. How they make decisions and why they make decisions are not the same, so your content and your mindset need to change too.

"More marketing = more new customers."

For some reason, people think that more marketing is the fastest way to grow their business. When, in reality, it is referrals and word of mouth that allow you to grow the fastest. This means making sure the customer experience (also known as the buyer's journey) is so great that they come back and tell others to join them. Finding new customers is harder and far more expensive than selling to existing or past customers, and the profitability margins of selling to existing customers are much higher too.

Stop here.

If you have not destroyed the limiting belief phrases page, find your inner Rebel and destroy it now!

CONGRATULATIONS! You have completed the first step toward empowering yourself to create marketing strategies that put your best foot forward and unleash your RebelMindset.

How did it feel to get rid of those limiting phrases? Write down the emotions and physical manifestations you experienced destroying that page with the limiting beliefs phrases:

_____

_____

Bonus point: What emoji best describes how you felt destroying that page? Circle one or two.

> **#RebelMindset: This is not a "read it and put it on the shelf" kind of book. This is a "roll up your sleeves and get $#@& done" kind of book, so grab your pen, pencil, crayon, or quill and let's get started!**

Are you ready?

PART I

Marketing Strategy

CHAPTER 1

The Rebel Reboot

"The best marketing is education."
— REGIS MCKENNA

CTL | ALT | DEL

You use this command to reboot your computer when it is freaking out on you, and you just want to start fresh. I need you to do the same with your brain and what you have learned about marketing up until now. We are refreshing and rebooting your marketing knowledge in this chapter.

Your first step in determining what your business needs is knowing what marketing consists of and how foundational strategies help your business grow. By understanding the basics, you will create better strategies, spend quality time on the right messaging, and, in the long run, spend less money on wasteful marketing.

If you are using the worksheets, go to rebelgirlmarketing.com/ guide and print out the PDF worksheet for Chapter 1. Go ahead, I'll be here when you get back.

Marketing Is a Team Sport

Engage your team. The creative process is best accomplished with others, not in a silo. The people who work with you have the same mission: happy customers and growing the business. As you go through this book, share what you've learned with your team. You never know where the next great idea will come from!

Have no employees? You can engage your network or mastermind group. Ask for their input on how you talk about your products/services and share the campaigns you create to make sure they make sense for your audience.

Whom can you invite to play on your marketing team?

Knowledge Is Power

Knowing the basic terms and concepts used to create your marketing strategies gives you the power to make better decisions on where and when to show up, what to say, and whom to say it to.

Here are some terms you may have heard along the way and ones you will be seeing throughout this book:

- B2B – businesses selling to other businesses (think professional services like bookkeeping)
- B2C – businesses selling to consumers (think retail)
- Brand – identifiable indicators for a specific person, organization, product, or service
- Branding – what you say about your brand, how your brand is perceived by others
- Business development – all activities related to both marketing and sales efforts
- CTA – Call to action – what you want people to do after engaging with your marketing
- CRM – Customer relationship management – software used to capture contact lists, send email blasts, track website usage, and track social media posts and engagement
- CX – this refers to the client experience, also known as the customer's journey – how easy or hard it is for your clients or customers to work with you, your products/service, and your team
- Customer – the person who buys from you (also known as the client)

- Digital footprint – anything you have that is found online: website, social media posts and profiles, and remote work
- Ecommerce – online stores that also take payments
- Ideal customer – the people willing and able to buy what you sell
- Keyword – specific words or phrases that a user enters in a search engine to find the desired information
- Lead – a company or person who has expressed interest and has the potential to become a customer
- Marketing channel – refers to the various ways you get your message out to the universe, such as social media, print advertising, TV ads, direct mail, etc.
- Prospect – a person or organization that is qualified to buy your product/service
- Target audience – where your ideal customer hangs out
- Team – anyone who represents you, including W2 and 1099 employees
- SEO – search engine optimization – the strategy used to increase traffic to your website by using keywords and phrases that people type in when using a search engine

This is just the tip of the proverbial iceberg when it comes to marketing terms, yet it is a solid start. Feel free to bookmark this page so you know where to find these definitions if you want to refer back to them later.

Q&A

When I tell people I am a marketing strategist, the one question I get over and over again is, "What the %$!&is marketing anyway?"

More French…and you thought this was only a marketing book…

That is literally how I have been asked that question by more than one frustrated business owner. I'm not kidding! With so many marketing channels to choose from, ways to tell your story, and audiences you want to reach, it can feel overwhelming…frustrating… impossible even.

The term marketing is sometimes confused with branding, so let's clear that confusion up immediately.

Marketing is something you do, an activity that elicits an action from the consumer. For example: you post an advertisement (marketing) for a sale on blue shoes at your store. As a result, the customers see your post and go to your website or come into your store to buy blue shoes (action).

> *If you need a more formal definition, the American Marketing Association[1] defines marketing as the activity, set of institutions, and processes for creating, communicating, delivering, and exchanging offerings that have value for customers, clients, partners, and society at large.*

Branding is part of the marketing strategy. The term *branding* is defined as giving meaning to your brand by shaping your identity in consumers' minds. Or as Jeff Bezos puts it, "*Branding is what people say about you when you are not in the room.*"

Don't worry, we will get to what defines a "brand" in the next section.

#RebelMindset Definition: Marketing is the action of letting your target audience know you exist, why you are awesome, and how to buy from you.

For now, let's continue our definition of marketing. The best way to describe what marketing is at its core is to talk about KNOW | LIKE | TRUST. Bob Burg coined this concept in his book *Endless Referrals*[2], first published in 1994. We will be using these three words throughout the book as they pertain to marketing.

---

[1] https://www.ama.org/the-definition-of-marketing-what-is-marketing/
[2] https://endlessreferrals.com/

Here is the basic premise for you to remember:

- KNOW = customers need to know you exist before they can buy from you (brand awareness)
- LIKE = customers who like what you say are more likely to buy from you (marketing content)
- TRUST = do customers trust you enough to buy from you? (selling process)

#RebelMindset: Marketing is KNOW and LIKE, while selling is taking them from LIKE to TRUST

How would you define marketing in your own words? Or which definition makes the most sense to you? Write it down so you can refer to it later in the book.

The next most popular question I get is, "What is my brand?"

A brand is a name, term, design, symbol (think logo), phrase, or any other element that identifies one product/service or organization/person versus the competition.

For example: Nike® and Adidas® are both sporting goods, shoes, apparel, etc., companies, yet their "brand" is the company's name, logo, trademarked taglines, color palettes, and the like. They use marketing to distribute the brand. Their *branding* provokes an emotional response in many, also known as customer loyalty. If you ask a person which is the better brand, many will have a definitive, passionate answer picking one brand over the other. It is almost like asking truck owners which is better, Ford or Chevy? But let's not go there... no need to start a rumble!

If you want the technical and slightly boring definition of a brand, here you go:

The formal definition of brand *refers to a business and marketing concept that helps people identify a particular company, product, or individual. Brands are intangible, which means you can't actually touch them; it's a matter of recognition or awareness. As such, they help shape people's perceptions of companies, their products, or individuals.*[3]

> **#RebelMindset: If <u>you</u> are the product or service, your name is the brand. If your <u>organization</u> is the product or service, the company name is the brand.**

Let's use everyday items as examples.
Tell me what this is:

Did you say, "facial tissue" or did you say, "Kleenex®"?
The *product* is facial tissue.
The *brand* is Kleenex® – there are numerous companies other than Kleenex® that makes facial tissues, yet Kleenex® is what people generally say when they need a tissue.(That is great marketing!)
Here is another one—what is this?

Did you say, "Cellphone" or maybe, "mobile phone"? That is the *product*.
Or did you say "iPhone®" or "Android®"? These are *brands*. Depending upon which one you use, that is probably how you answered.

What is the name of your brand? We will be discussing products/ services in Chapter 2, so for now just write down your brand name(s). Side note: Only concentrate on what is seen by the outside

---

[3] https://www.investopedia.com/terms/b/brand.asp

world, not how your bookkeeper or the IRS identifies you (i.e., umbrella companies).

Now that we've identified the difference between marketing and branding, let's talk about what makes up a good marketing strategy. Remember, marketing is simply storytelling. Your marketing strategy defines the what, how, when, why, and whom you tell that story to.

What Is a Marketing Strategy?

Your marketing strategy is simply the *plan* to promote and sell your product or service.

KNOW: Our first task is to create brand awareness. To do that, we need to dip into our psychology bag of tricks. Did you know that on average someone needs to engage with your brand five to seven times[4] before they will remember it?

To create brand awareness, I like to start with the 3Cs: consistency, channels, and cognitive. By knowing how the 3Cs create engagement with your target audience, it allows you to make better decisions on where to spend your time and money.

In my opinion when creating your strategy, the No. 1 rule is consistency.

1. **CONSISTENCY**. Doing something once will most likely not be remembered. Consistency in your marketing will increase brand awareness over time. Don't "Post & Pray" – meaning post once on social media and pray someone will see it.

   In the beginning, it is a guessing game. You can never know exactly when people will engage with your marketing until you do it for a while. Over time, the digital data is collected so you can review the insights and analytics to determine when people engaged with your marketing.

---

[4] https://www.smallbizgenius.net/by-the-numbers/branding-statistics/

Some examples of audience actions data analytics will tell you who:

- viewed your social post
- opened your email
- clicked on a link
- visited your website

... you get the picture.

This is where using a marketing platform like a CRM, email automation product, and Google Analytics is useful to collect the data and provide the analytical results over time. These platforms will tell you what day and time your audience engaged with you so you can determine the best time to post, email, or add new information to your website.

Whatever channel you use, do it with consistency.

> **#RebelMindset: Posting will not make you rich, yet consistently staying in front of your target audience builds awareness over time.**

2. **CHANNELS.** There are different marketing channels you can utilize to effectively appeal to your audience. Using a mix of channels helps to build your brand awareness. Which channel you use will depend on where your target audience hangs out. (Hold tight: In Chapter 4 we will be diving deeper into understanding where your customers hang out.)

For now, here are some commonly used channels:

- **Catalog.** Catalog direct is a marketing channel where a potential customer browses through a printed or digital catalog. A catalog may include prices, product descriptions, or images of the options. This channel can eliminate the need to interact with a potential customer face-to-face.

- **Digital advertisements.** Digital is best for companies that sell products through a website. You can buy advertisement space on social media platforms, other websites, or use your own social media platforms to market to your specific following. Think pop-up ads or banners on a website.

- **Direct mail.** Using demographics and geographic data, printed mailings are sent to targeted households or businesses to inform the owners of products or services available in their communities.

- **Email marketing.** Promotional emails are sent to a target audience that contain a specific message. A marketing email may include information about an upcoming sale, a new product release, or changes to a familiar product.

- **Events.** You can host an event yourself or attend an organized event, such as an industry conference. These events provide the opportunity for potential customers to directly ask questions about your product or service, understand its value, and potentially make a purchase.

- **Networking.** Representing your organization at a networking event to build professional relationships can be done in person or virtually. The common goal is to help others and build brand awareness.

- **Search engine optimization (SEO) marketing.** SEO refers to the results that a potential customer sees when searching for something online using keywords, resulting in higher traffic on your company's website. Work with your web developer to strategically use keywords throughout your website.

- **Social media.** There seem to be a endless number of social media channels to choose from these days. Knowing the demographics of your audience will determine which social media channels are the best ones to spend your time and money on.

This is not an exhaustive list. Once you know where your target audience hangs out, you can determine which channel(s) you could use.

📄 Place a checkmark next to the channels you are currently using. List any other channels you use in the blank spots.

> **#RebelMindset: By mixing up channels, you mix up how your audience digests your information. Using a combination of the five senses increases your chances of being remembered.**

3. **COGNITION.** You can build brand awareness by using the five senses. Your senses are tied to emotions and emotions are tied to memory. Customers remember your marketing when it provokes emotion.

   o Sight – color, images, text, graphics, video
      ■ Using the same color palette and logo on all of your marketing increases brand recognition by 80 percent[5] – find something you love and stick with it! According to *Forbes*[6], presenting brand consistency across all marketing platforms can increase revenue by up to 23 percent.
      ■ When you physically show up at networking events on a consistent basis, it will help with brand recognition and create a sense of trust and familiarity to other members.
      ■ EXAMPLE: When I say "brown" what company comes to mind? (most people will think: UPS®.)
   o Sound – one voice for audio ads/voice-overs, sound effects, theme music
      ■ Using the same voice for videos and radio ads also helps with brand recognition. Organizations often use one spokesperson or actor for their television ads. Sometimes you don't even need to be looking at your TV when an

---

[5] https://www.smallbizgenius.net/by-the-numbers/branding-statistics/
[6] https://www.forbes.com/sites/gabrielshaoolian/2018/08/10/10-marketing-web-design-branding-statistics-to-help-you-prioritize-business-growth-initiatives/?sh=17adb563d708

ad comes on to recognize the voice and often the brand associated with it.

- Your voice will again be recognized when you are consistent in your networking efforts.
- EXAMPLE: brand jingles. I bet dollars to donuts that you can sing these words and know the brand: "They're magically delicious!" (Lucky Charms®) or I bet you can finish this one, "Give me a break, give me a break, break me off a piece of that ..." (KitKat®).

o Touch – soft, rough, metallic, wood, wet, dry
- Printed collateral: Is your paper collateral simply printed on 8.5x11 paper? Or does it have a unique shape, thickness, and texture to it?
- Branded giveaways like pens, journals, stress balls, and phone accessories are common items that offer tactile sensory impressions with your audience.
- If it makes sense, utilizing hands-on experiences is a great way to showcase the quality of your product.
- EXAMPLE: Go to any clothing store and before you try anything on, feel the fabric first. Think cotton vs wool. Or when mortgage companies send direct mail to their customers. One mailer is a standard rectangular postage-size envelope, while another is made of thicker paper and dye cut into the shape of a house. Which one is more likely to catch your attention and get opened first?

o Smell – sweet, woody, citrus, pungent, mint, savory (to name a few)
- Scents can be strongly tied to emotions. Using scents and fragrances to either calm or excite your audience is especially good for brick & mortar locations – it all depends upon how you want them to act when they get there.
- EXAMPLE: Aspa uses calming scents like lavender or eucalyptus to relax their customers as they walk in.

Meanwhile, a restaurant will use savory and sweet scents to turn on diners' taste buds.

○ Taste – mmmmm… fooooooood… in your best Homer Simpson voice

  ■ This would be for those of you in the food and beverage industry…obviously.

  ■ EXAMPLE: How many times have you come home from the grocery store or a big-box store with items that you never intended to buy because you tried a sample and loved it?

The key is to use a variety of ways to get your brand in front of and remembered by your target audience.

> **#RebelMindset: Get creative! One of my customers gives away unique candy selections at expos, drawing in the curiosity of their network to their booth at each convention. (BTW: They are in construction, not food/beverage.)**

Use the worksheet for this chapter to check off all the senses that your product/service can use to create brand awareness.

Marketing 101: The 4Ps of the Marketing Mix… and a few more…

The 4Ps of Marketing have been around since the 1950s (popularized by McCarthy, 1960)[7] and have been used by marketing professionals ever since. In future chapters we will dive into each one of the 4Ps, but for now let's just go over the basics of what each one is all about.

- **Product** – (includes services) what you sell, simple enough.

---

[7] https://www.investopedia.com/terms/f/four-ps.asp#:~:text=Neil%20Borden%20popularized%20the%20idea,advertising%20professor%20at%20Harvard%20University.

- **Price** – how much your product or service costs. Caveat: what value does the customer perceive to be getting for that price?
- **Place** – where you can buy your product or service.
- **Promotion** – how you let people outside of your organization know what you have to sell.

The Extra 3Ps: An additional three elements were added to the Marketing Mix that help us meet the challenges of marketing services, *People, Process, and Physical Evidence* (Booms & Bitner, 1982)

- **People** – having the right people on your business development team is essential. They will be building your brand identity, creating brand awareness, representing you and your organization as well as fulfilling the customers' requests.
- **Processes** – Better known in marketing as the customer journey or client experience (CX), the process is all about delivering what you promised.
- **Physical evidence** – Almost all services include some physical elements, even if the bulk of what the consumer is paying for is intangible. Physical evidence in a service-based product could be a website, business card, meeting summary report, increased revenue, reduced turnover, and the like.

📄 Write down how you would describe each of these 7Ps as it pertains to your current marketing. We will dive deeper into each of these Ps later in the book, so don't freak out if you are having trouble jotting something down. (That's why you are here.)

Inspired or Confused?

We have come to the end of Chapter 1. Either you feel like you have a good baseline understanding of marketing or this book is headed to your burn pile. As we go through the rest of the book, you may want to refer to this chapter for a refresher on terms and concepts.

Review Your RebelMindset

- Marketing is what you do…branding is what people say about you.
- KNOW & LIKE is marketing… going from LIKE to TRUST is selling.
- Be consistent, mix your channels' and use the senses and be remembered.

Chapter 1 Worksheet Content:

- Whom can you invite to play on your marketing team?

  _____

  _____

- How do you define marketing?

  _____

  _____

- What is the name of your brand? We will be discussing products/ services in Chapter 2, so for now just write down your brand name(s).
- Place a checkmark next to each channel you feel will benefit your customers. There are blank rows for other channels you may be using; write them in. For the channels you are already using, are you utilizing them consistently?

Channel	Use Now?	Use in Future?
Catalog		
Digital advertisements		
Direct mail		
Direct selling		
Email marketing		
Events		
Networking		
Search Engine Optimization (SEO)		

- Which of the 5 senses can you use in your marketing?
    - Sight
    - Smell
    - Sound
    - Touch
    - Taste
- How do each of the 7Ps pertain to you and your organization?
    - Product / Service
    - Price
    - Place
    - Promotion
    - People
    - Processes
    - Physical Evidence

7 PS OF MARKETING

PRODUCT/SERVICE
QUALITY
PACKAGING

PEOPLE
TEAM MEMBERS
CUSTOMER SERVICE

PROMOTION
ADVERTISEMENT
CAMPAIGN

PHYSICAL EVIDENCE
FACILITIES
REPORTS

PLACE
RETAIL
E-COMMERCE

PRICE
VALUE BASED
ACTUAL COST

PROCESS
OFFERINGS
SERVICE DELIVERY

CHAPTER 2

Stop Committing Random Acts of Marketing

"Rowing harder doesn't help if the boat is headed in the wrong direction."
—KENICHI OHMAE

If you are in Ohio and want to go see the Grand Canyon, you don't start driving east! You may get there eventually but it will take you a whole lot longer and cost you a lot more money. In the same manner, more marketing won't fix your lack of quality leads if you are pointing your marketing in the wrong direction.

Reminder: you can use the space at the end of this chapter to customize you learning or go to rebelgirlmarketing.com/ guide to print your Chapter 2 worksheet.

Start With the End in Mind

You don't plan a road trip with no destination in mind. Well, maybe you do. When it comes to your marketing, that's not exactly a great idea. Where do you want your marketing to take you?

> **#RebelMindset: Spending time and money on marketing simply because you were told that's what you need to do is, well...a *waste* of time and money!**

Why do you need marketing? What are the goals you're trying to reach?

- Is it to raise brand awareness?
- Is it to gain new customers?
- Is it to retain or upsell existing customers?
- Are you launching a new product or service?
- Are you establishing yourself as a subject matter expert?
- Are you growing your team?

You could say "YES!" to all the above. Please don't.

It's better to simply pick one or two to start with for the sake of your own sanity and for the sake of your audience. Nothing can kill a brand faster than spending time and money on marketing that makes no sense and tries to be too many things to too many people. Trust me.

Knowing *why* you need marketing in the first place gives you clarity and focus.

If you are still unsure of the reason you need marketing, here is where I need you to channel your inner three-year-old and ask yourself "why" over and over and over again until you have a clear understanding of where you want your marketing to take you and your organization.

Let's look at these same questions from above, just using the "why?" perspective:

- Why do I need to raise brand awareness?
  - o Does my competition have too much of the market share?
  - o Is my business new and nobody knows I exist yet?
- Why do I need new customers?
  - o Do I have capacity that needs to be filled?
  - o Am I losing existing customers to the competition?
- Why do I need to retain and/or upsell existing customers?
  - o Is there more I can do for them, and they just don't know it?
  - o Have they outgrown what they currently buy, and I have a better solution?

- Am I for consistency?
    - Why does anyone care about this new product/service?
    - Why am I launching it now? Seasonal/market change/new technology?
- Why do I want to be established as a subject matter expert?
    - Do I want to be paid for my expertise for speaking or writing?
    - Is my knowledge sought after as an outsourced expert for organizations?
- Why do I need to grow my team for consistency?
    - Are I at capacity and need help to support customers?
    - Are I expanding into another area that we need an expert for?

Remember, you can have more than one reason you want to develop marketing strategies. Yet, focusing on one or two at a time is a great way to avoid being overwhelmed and frustrated with your marketing efforts.

Go to the end of this chapter or to your PDF and mark one or two of the most immediate reasons you are developing your marketing. You can also mark any of the other reasons that you will focus on in the future. Be sure answer the question "why" that reason is your focus; it will help you in the chapters ahead as you develop your target audience and marketing content.

> **#RebelMindset: It's time to stop throwing your marketing against the wall to see if it will stick. Don't skip this step; choose one or two reasons why you need marketing.**

Focus Areas

<u>Raise Brand Awareness or Gain New Customers:</u>
Increasing your brand awareness and seeking new customers is the most common reason organizations build their marketing strategy. Customers come and go, it's simply the nature of business.

Before anyone can become a customer, they need to KNOW you exist! Building your brand awareness is vital to regularly gaining new customers. The audience you are marketing to may not need what you sell the moment they see your brand, yet consistency in your marketing (#1 of the 3Cs) puts your brand top of mind when the need arises.

Let's play a little game to drive this concept home. Write down the first brand you think of for the following categories:

Automobile: _____

Hardware Store: _____

Fast Food: _____

Laundry Detergent: _____

Copier: _____

Ice Cream: _____

It may have been a while since you bought some of these products, yet you have a brand that is top of mind. And, you might have even listed a brand that you don't even buy.

BTW: if you are going out for ice cream, I'll take some Breyer's® Salted Caramel. Thanks!

The challenge is that, on average, a person needs anywhere between five and 12 impressions of your brand before they remember it. The solution is that creating the right marketing strategies greatly improves the chances of your brand being remembered! And that's why you are here.

> *It's important to pause here to explain what an **"impression"** is as it pertains to marketing. Just like when you first meet someone, there is an immediate "impression." This is true in marketing too. An "impression" is an idea, feeling, or opinion about something or someone formed without conscious thought.*

Retaining and upselling to existing customers

Here's a statistic[1] that will get your attention: Acquiring a NEW customer can cost seven times more than retaining an existing customer. SEVEN TIMES MORE!!

I'm gonna let that sink in for a moment. Breathe...

This marketing strategy is missed by a large number of businesses today. Once we have someone as a customer, we tend to move onto the next new sale. Existing customers already KNOW you and hopefully they also LIKE you and TRUST you enough to buy from you. Yet will they do it again?

If you are still not convinced this is an important strategy, let me hit you with a few more mind-blowing statistics[2]:

- When selling to an existing customer, you have a 60-70 percent chance of successfully closing the sale vs. only 5-20 percent chance of closing a new customer sale.
- AND as if that weren't enough, by increasing customer retention by only 5 percent, it can increase your profits by over 25 percent!
- Okay, one more statistic for you, and if you don't get psyched out by this one, check your pulse. Loyal customers spend 67 percent more than new ones.

BOOM! Mic drop.

The No. 1 strategy to upselling an existing customer is communication...clear, consistent, value-based communication. This doesn't mean filling their email inbox with offers, it means staying in touch, so you are top of mind when a need again arises for your product/service. Timing is everything too. If your product is consumable, reaching out just before they need more is the perfect time to connect with your existing customers. Happy existing customers are also likely to

---

[1] https://www.markinblog.com/customer-loyalty-retention-statistics/
[2] https://www.markinblog.com/customer-loyalty-retention-statistics/

tell others how awesome you are; this is called word-of-mouth advertising.

When is your product or service needed again? Knowing this and making it super easy to buy from you again is the key to keeping and upselling existing customers.

For example: High-end clothing stores use email, direct mail, and digital selling to stay in front of customers with offers like, "Spend $XXX and get XX percent off," using the known quality of their products and the status of their brand as their main selling points. They are selling to people who they know are willing to spend more money on clothing. They will also offer discounts if you refer a new customer their way. This is known as brand-loyalty marketing.

New Product/Service Launch

This tactic is all about hype! If you are launching a new product or service, it's about building momentum BEFORE it is available. This increases the likelihood people will want it and not want to miss out, you know…FOMO! (That means fear of missing out for those of you living under a rock.)

#RebelMindset: Get excited about it, build the anticipation, and give the audience a glimpse of why they need it by show casing a feature or two before it is available.

The second half of this strategy is making absolutely sure you can fill the order requests as you advertise it. If you don't, your customers will be disappointed like you just popped all their balloons at their birthday party. This will negatively affect your brand and worst of all, they will tell their friends and anyone else who will listen why they shouldn't buy from you.

Think of a movie trailer…a movie is promoted months before it is released. How well the promo is received and how often it is played on the various marketing channels will determine its opening weekend success or failure.

Pro Tip: As you build out your new product or service, build your launch strategy so you are prepared to advertise and sell when the new product/service is ready.

<u>SME: Subject Matter Expert</u>
You are an expert in whatever product/service you sell, your target audience is not. This means you do not create content using industry jargon and acronyms in your marketing. Your marketing is simply storytelling and showing your audience how you solve their problems. Use more detailed information and content during the sales process once you have their interest in you and your organization.

There are two main ways you can show up as a SME:

- Writing
  - When writing your own content, be sure to have someone proofread your writing. In writing this book, I started with a "shitty first draft" (advice taken from the book: <u>Bird by Bird</u>, written by Anne Lamott), then listened to it with the "read aloud" feature in WORD and edited it along the way…then sent it to my lovely editor, Claudia…then another round of editing with the "read aloud" feature…then I sent it to a few honest friends in my network (HONEST friends, don't be afraid of constructive feedback!)…then another round of editing…then it was ready for submitting to the publisher. The point: Your first draft is rarely your final draft! Take your time; don't rush the writing process.
  - You don't like writing? That's okay. You can use a content writer or ghostwriter to get the article/blog to a format for publication. PRO TIP: Use voice recognition software, like otter.ai, to convert audio to text or you can use your phone or computer to record audio and send that file to the content writer. All you need to do is speak; no typing needed.
  - Once you have an article or blog done, you can use it in many different channels:
    - Industry publications
    - Social media groups

- Your social media page(s)
- Website
- Speaking engagements
    - You can also break what you wrote into smaller sections and share them in a series of posts or articles.

> **#RebelMindset: It's not about you. Writing is about telling a story, capturing their attention, and showing how you solve problems for others.**

"Content marketing is really like a first date. If all you do is talk about yourself, there won't be a second date."
—DAVID BEEBE

- Speaking
    - Speaking at conferences, networking groups, or being a guest on a podcast is great exposure, both as a subject matter expert and for brand recognition.
    - When creating content and presentations for your speaking topics, be sure to practice your speech on others before you present it to your audience. Gather a group of people who you know will be honest with you and give you feedback that is constructive and helpful.
    - ALWAYS REMEMBER: *You* are the presentation the audience came to hear, while the slides or handouts you pull together are there only to support your content. There is a reason some presentations are called "death by PowerPoint."

> **#RebelMindset: A poor speaking presentation is the opposite of good marketing.**

PRO TIP 1: Get some training on how to speak professionally before you take to the stage. At a minimum, do your presentation in front of a very honest person who will tell you if you suck.

PRO TIP 2: Record your presentation when practicing – audio and video! I do this for all my new topics. I record myself giving the presentation and review it for content, my personal presentation style, and for where to include audience engagement. I can tell you this helps tremendously, and I have saved many audiences from tortuously boring talks!

One time when I was reviewing my recording of a presentation, I started to laugh out loud! I saw myself getting really animated with my body movement and it looked like I was trying to land a plane! Once I stopped laughing, that video was quickly deleted from my computer… I kind of wish I still had it for a blooper reel!

Time is Money: Spend Wisely

Most organizations have busy times and slow times of the year. Planning two to three months ahead at a minimum is the key to less stress and more fun when it comes to your marketing efforts. During your higher revenue-generating months, set aside funds to spend on marketing during the slower months. Remember, consistency keeps your brand in front of your audience so when they need what you sell, they think of you first.

Like the title of this chapter, it's easy to find yourself committing random acts of marketing. Here's what usually happens: When you have a full customer load, your marketing tends to stop. Then, when your customer load is light, you find your sales funnel is empty and there are no prospects. Sound familiar?

Yes, marketing takes time and time is money. So, if you are spending time on your marketing instead of time working with customers or worse, not spending time with family and friends and enjoying life, then it is time to outsource your marketing. There are plenty of ways to outsource your marketing without spending all your profits on a big, fancy marketing agency. With the influx of entrepreneurs, you can find someone in your network who will help free up your time and keep your brand in front of your audience. It will be money well spent!

Speaking of Money: How Much?

I have been putting this off long enough. It's time to talk about the "B" word: budget. There is no hard and fast rule for what amount to budget for marketing. I have seen articles list anywhere from 1.5 percent to 5 percent of annual revenue as the standard measure to budget for marketing.

Take out your worksheet. On there you will find a space to write what you spent in the past three years for marketing. You can use your tax forms to help you find the numbers if you don't already know them. Figure out what percentage of total revenue you spent on marketing. What did you spend the most money on (i.e.,: printed material, brand redesign, new website, expo booth materials, meals, sponsorship, etc.)? What amount are you comfortable spending to move your business forward? As we move through this book, keep that number in mind.

> **#RebelMindset:** It's not a budget as much as it is an investment in your brand's future. ROI doesn't stand for Return on BUDGET, it's INVESTMENT!

Part of establishing your investment is to track what works. If you are tracking your marketing spend, hopefully you are also tracking which marketing channel each new customer came from. For example: You spend $400 on a membership to your local chamber. Did you receive over $400 in referrals from that chamber? Tracking what you spend in comparison to how much business you received from that marketing channel is how you track the ROI.

Reminder: *It takes five-12 times for your target audience to remember your brand.*

Reality check: Marketing is not always trackable. Let's use an ad in a printed publication as our example. You cannot track how many people saw your ad, nor can you track how many people stopped to read your ad. Yet, that advertisement adds to the number of times your target audience is exposed to your brand. If someone tells you they contacted you because of that ad, then it is trackable. Placing an ad in a publication your target audience reads as part of your overall marketing strategy is just one stop in your customer's journey.

Here is where you may need to take a pause. Breathe.

Go to the worksheet associated with Chapter 2 and see where you may have some gaps. Do you know why you need marketing? What areas that we talked about apply to what you can include in your marketing? What is your biggest takeaway from this chapter? What questions do you still have?

Storytime!

To round out this chapter, let me tell you the story of my friend Dawn Jacques, the founder of Milwaukee Paws Pet Care, a pet walking and pet care service. This organization is not just any ordinary pet walking service. Dawn and her team go above and beyond to make sure their customer's journey (both pet owner and fur baby) is extraordinary.

Dawn's current marketing strategy is pointed to two specific areas where she is looking to grow:

1. Gain new customers
2. Upsell and increase engagement with existing customers

Dawn uses social media, Google Ads, and word of mouth as her primary marketing channels. The key to her success in these areas is letting her team members help! Dawn is an expert in canine training, not social media.

#RebelMindset: Remember, marketing is a team sport!

JOURNEY

INTERACTION

CHANNEL

METHOD OF INTERACTION

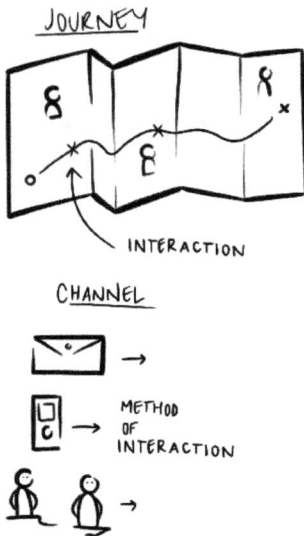

Let's start with social media. If a picture is worth a thousand words, then photos of a cute puppy are worth 10 million words in my opinion, and I'm a cat person! Using social media to post photos of the dogs Milwaukee Paws is walking or training (with the owner's permission, of course) is perfect! The owners get to see their pets and animal lovers get to see how happy their furry customers are with the services Milwaukee Paws has to offer. Dawn also provides pro tips within her posts so she can show how she is a subject matter expert. She uses still photos as well as video to capture the audience's attention. With each post she shows the company logo in the corner of the photo. Social media plays a huge part in her marketing based on her industry: pets.

Social media helps with both of her growth objectives. People who pause to check out the cute pet photos may have a pet of their own and see the logo on the post, which increases brand awareness. Brand awareness increases the chance that they will search for Milwaukee Paws when looking for a pet sitter or dog walker. The same goes for upselling existing customers. By posting pro tips, current customers will learn about the different services Dawn and her team offer, increasing the likelihood of buying more services from Milwaukee Paws. Social media also makes it very easy to engage with the audience by liking and sharing cute pet photos.

This marketing channel costs one precious commodity: time. As a business owner, you may very well have a better way to spend your time other than on social media platforms. Whom do you know that can help you?

Next, we'll talk about Google Ads.[3] (formally known as Google AdWords) This marketing channel is a pay-per-click (or PPC) product. Google Ads are found at the top of your search results. have **Ad** next to the title of the search result, (at least they did when I wrote this book in 2022), and have shown to dramatically increase the traffic to your website…for a price. Every time someone clicks on that ad, you pay. Hence, pay per click.

Dawn uses PPC advertising to drive traffic to her website when her target audience is searching for pet sitting, dog walking, dog training, or any other number of keywords she uses in her Google Ad PPC program. For her business, this is the best way for her to find new customers.

Finally, let's talk about word-of-mouth (pun intended…) marketing. Dawn includes referral rewards as a part of this program. The best people to spread the word about your organization are your happy customers and team members!! For each referral, a current customer receives a percentage off of their next invoice. Each team member who refers a new customer receives a percentage of the first month's invoice as a bonus.

If you don't have a defined referral program, this may be a gap, or it could just not be a viable option. Gifts instead of money are a great way to say thank you! (WARNING: Be sure to check with your industry standards for limitations that may fall under the "rebating" statute of gift giving – for example, some financial industries limit gift giving and receiving to under $25). If you are not allowed to give discounts or gifts, then a handwritten thank-you note (NOT an email) is a great option. Handwritten notes are always a good idea! Word-of-mouth marketing is ideal for gaining new customers.

This is not the whole story of Dawn's marketing strategy. I simply wanted you to see how focusing on one or two reasons you need

---

[3] https://www.hallaminternet.com/google-adwords-pros-and-cons/

marketing in the first place allows you to create strategic lead generating content vs committing random acts of marketing.

Thank you, Dawn for letting me share your marketing strategy in this book! Check out her pet-sitting services at: milwaukeepaws.com.

Review Your RebelMindset

- Know why you need marketing
- It's an investment, not a budget
- Marketing is a team sport; who's on your team?

Chapter 2 worksheet content:

Why do you need marketing?

Reason	Immediate Need	Future Need	Why do I need to focus on this?
Brand Awareness			
New Customers			
Upsell existing customers			
Launching a new product or service			
Establishing yourself as a subject matter expert			
Grow your team			
Other:			

Budget:

Year	Last Year: 20_____	2 Years Ago: 20_____	3 Years Ago: 20_____
Total Spend on Marketing	$	$	$
Percentage of Total Revenue:	%	%	%
Highest Amount On:			
Willing to Spend in 20_____ $			

Q&A:

- Why you need marketing?
- What areas discussed apply to your potential marketing plan?
- What is your biggest takeaway from this chapter?
- What other questions do you have?

Pro Tip: You may be thinking you have no time for all of this and it's only the end of Chapter 2! I suggest two books (to read after this one, of course!)

- *Who Not How* by Dan Sullivan talks about the power of delegation.
- *Atomic Habits* by James Clear is jam packed with great advice on how to get more out of your day.

You can thank me later!

CHAPTER 3

What Are You *Really* Selling?

*"Quality in a service or product is not what you put into it.
It is what the client or customer gets out of it."*
—PETER F. DRUCKER

You might be tempted to skip this chapter, assuming you already know your product. Stick with me; there are likely some things you haven't thought about yet. I know it sounds silly to ask you to identify what you sell. Yet…what you sell is not just a product or service, it is so much more! You sell solutions and with solutions come emotions.

Friendly reminder: go to rebelgirlmarketing. com/guide and print out Chapter 3s worksheet. If you only print out one worksheet… this is the one!

Solving your customers' problems triggers an emotion within your customer and within you. Those emotions are what people buy from, not the features and benefits of what you sell.

> **#RebelMindset: "Do my product/service names and definitions make sense to my audience or just to me?"**

As professionals, we want to sound smart, so we give our products and services convoluted, catchy, or complicated names. I have met a lot of business owners who have not taken the time to clearly identify their product/service in terms that their customers can understand.

That is what this chapter is about: seeing what you sell from the customers' perspective.

Start with Marketing Mix Ps #1 Product and #2 Price

In Chapter 1, we talked about the 7Ps of the Marketing Mix. In this chapter we are starting with understanding our product/service and price strategies.

Product vs. Service

A product is a tangible item sold (think office supplies) whereas a service is intangible (think consultant). You can sell both at the same time (think auto mechanic – he sells the parts and the service to put those parts in your vehicle).

📄 Do you sell a product, service, or both?

Go to the back of this chapter or grab your Chapter 3 worksheet and write down the general category your products or services fall under. For example: consulting, supplier, contractor, accounting, nursing, mechanic, engineering, professional services, education, not-for-profit, etc.

Then get a little more specific and add subcategories. I'll use the samples above as the example: **marketing** consulting, **industrial parts** supplier, **tax** accounting, **oncology** nursing, **large engine** mechanic, **legal** professional services, **higher** education, **children's** not-for-profit, etc.

📄 With the absolute understanding that you may have several categories and/or subcategories, take some time and write down what they are for your organization. Go ahead, I'll wait here.

Welcome back!

To understand what you *really* sell, answer the following questions about what you offer your customers. If you are not sure how to answer them, it's okay! That's why you picked up this book in the first place. I simply need you to stop seeing your products/services from a features and benefits perspective and see what you sell from the customers' perspective.

Go to the back of this chapter or your worksheet and answer the following questions for each subcategory of product or service. Before you do that…

#REBELMINDSET: Write your answers to these questions as if you are standing in front of a 12th grade class on Career Day. How would you describe what you do to them?

---

1. What problems do your product/service solve for your customers?
2. What emotions are tied to solving the problems?
3. What features does it have to meet these needs?
4. What are the benefits of those features?
5. Where can the customer buy your product or service?
6. How and where will the customer use it?
7. How is it different from your competitors' products/services?

As an example, here are answers I may give for my own business.

Example Answers: Marketing Consulting
1. Creating customized marketing strategies for businesses without a marketing person on staff as well as training small business owners about marketing basics.
2. Confidence, less stress, less worry, pride in how their organization is being represented.
3. Sales and marketing expertise, a network of vendors to provide specialized services as needed (i.e.,: web design, SEO, Google Ads, etc.). Written short-term and long-term strategies and marketing mindset training for the business owner and team.

4. Faster launch to intentional marketing strategies vs. trying to learn marketing on their own or onboarding a marketing team member. Implementation of customized strategies that connect with the right audience, at the right time, with the right messaging.
5. Contact me directly for consulting pricing and contract or eLearning available at rebelgirlmarketing.com.
6. Work directly with customers and their team – in person or via virtual calls for as long as they need me. Training provided builds long-term skill sets in both sales and marketing functions.
7. My experience in both sales and marketing in the corporate world allows me to see both sides of business development strategies, how to market, and how to sell.

We will be using the answers to these questions in later chapters, I promise! You are not wasting your time.

If you need help, enlist your team members and ask how they would answer these questions when talking with a customer.

Don't rush through this part. I'll be here when you get back.

> **#RebelMindset: Read what you wrote aloud; it helps to hear what you are trying to tell others. It usually sounds good in your head, yet reading it aloud gives it a whole new perspective.**

What You REALLY Sell

You may think you are only selling a product or service, yet you offer so much more! You sell solutions.

What most people don't consider when creating their marketing is how much emotion is tied to the solutions you sell and the buying process. In the previous section, you listed the problems you solve and some of the emotions that are triggered when you solve that problem.

To dive a little deeper into the emotional aspect of your marketing, below you will find eight basic emotions and their opposites, developed by the Robert Plutchik Group. Feel free to go back to the last section and review the emotions you listed. Did you miss one?

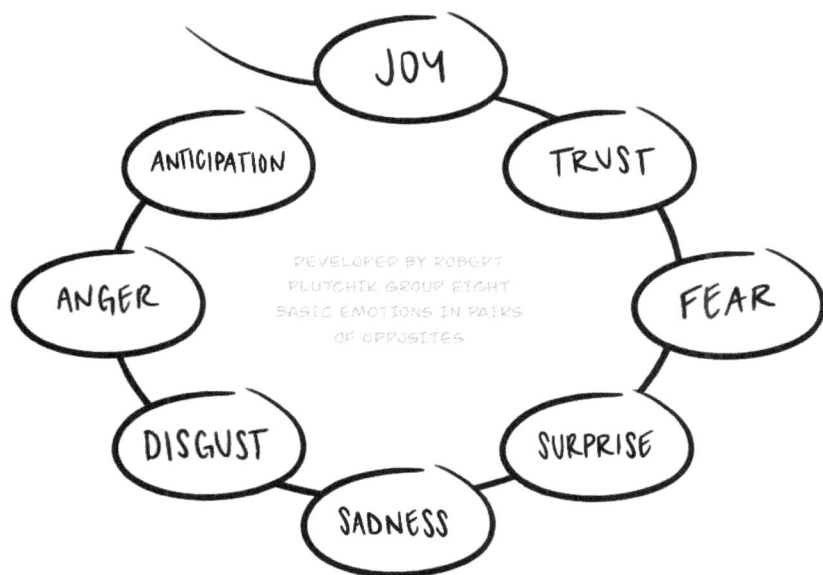

Under each of these eight basic emotions, you can have any number of emotions that are tied to it. Let's take fear as an example. When someone is fearful, it triggers the flight–or–fight response. I'd like to add one more: freeze. Today we don't just run or get defensive, sometimes we do nothing out of fear. In business, fear is one of the most common problems solved when selling a product or service. What are your customers afraid of that you can resolve?

There are seven common fears, according to an article by Shivali Anand[1] in an Early Growth blog: Which one of these fears can you relate to your customer base?

---

[1] https://earlygrowthfinancialservices.com/blog/7-common-entrepreneurial-fears-and-how-to-overcome-them-early-growth/

1. Fear of failure: This is a powerful obstacle preventing us from embracing opportunities and taking action that has unknown outcomes. Failure is oftentimes connected to ego and pride. Yet, failure is an unavoidable part of being in business! We will all fail at some point. You can let it stop you, or you can learn from it. The choice is yours.

2. Fear of change: It is easy to get into a routine of how you do things day to day, even if you know it is not the most efficient use of your time. When it comes to overcoming the fear of change, knowledge is power. It is easier to make changes when you understand if taking the next step is worth the risk, which brings us to #3.

3. Fear of taking risks: In most cases, to take your business to the next level, you need to take a few risks, such as: hiring someone, investing in technology, learning a new skill, etc. There is no guarantee it will pay off, yet you know that if you don't take that risk, you will not grow. Again, this is where knowledge is power. Gather as much information as you can so you turn your fear into a plan.

4. Fear of uncertainty: This is a crazy world we are living in; there is so much uncertainty that watching too much news will put you under your covers for days! When uncertainty is the fear, focus on what you can influence or control and let the rest go. My kids get so sick of me saying this to them, yet following the philosophy of only focusing on what I can influence or control, has allowed me to move forward in my work and in my life faster and with more joy than when I only focused on the "what ifs?!?!" in my life.

5. Fear of not being good enough: Not only can our customers relate to this one...I can almost guarantee you have felt this same fear. The question you need to ask yourself is: "What does good enough mean?" This is your limiting belief rearing its ugly head! Tell him/her to shut the @#$% up and go away! My friend Krista Morrissey is a life coach and she taught me a lesson that has kept this fear at bay for me. The lesson: *Your only competition is yourself from yesterday.* That means that the only person I compare myself to is who I was the day before. Am I a better person today? What can

I do to improve areas I need to focus on? Where are the gaps in my services and how do I fill them?

> **#RebelMindset: You. Are. Enough. If someone is telling you otherwise, they need to take a good, long, hard look in the mirror. Usually, they are the ones who feel inadequate and are casting their fear onto you.**

6. Fear of letting others down: There are so many people who rely on you. I get it! This fear is a weight that all business professionals bear, and the list is long: family, friends, team members, bosses, investors, customers, vendors, and ourselves. Reality check: We cannot please everyone. Each circumstance presents its own balance of whom you can satisfy and whom you cannot. Knowing who is the most important person in each situation is important, and you should be ready to handle whatever repercussions you may face with those you may disappoint.

7. Fear of success: This fear sounds counterintuitive, yet it is very, very real! We all define "success" differently, yet this fear relates back to several of the other fears:
   a. #6 - feeling like once you are successful, you won't be enough.
   b. You like being safe and going along at the pace you are at now, which relates back to #2, the fear of change.
   c. Suddenly, you are in demand. Now what? #4, the fear of uncertainty.

Which one(s) can you relate to? Which one(s) do your customers relate to? How does your product/service mitigate that fear? What can you say to your customers that will help reduce their fear(s) and move them further down the sales funnel?

In your selling process, one of the most powerful sales tools you have is being able to mitigate your customers' fear with knowledge. Educating your customers on how you work, and what the expected outcomes are, and answering their questions will reduce their fears and you will be closer to closing the sale.

> **#Rebelmindset: I am not and will not ever suggest you sell by causing fear in your customers; only by eliminating their fears are you truly selling a solution.**

Pause here.

Take a deep breath, shake out your arms and legs, and maybe take a pause to reset your mind. Focusing on fear can lead us down a path we do not want to go down, so pause and regroup. I'll be here when you get back.

> *"FEAR is an acronym in the English language*
> *for 'False Evidence Appearing Real'."*
> —NEALE DONALD WALSCH

Differentiation as a Strategy

When it is time to make a buying decision, the customer has a choice between you and someone else. Why should they choose you? Here is where we create your unique selling proposition. Simply put, it's a statement that explains what differentiates you from your competition.

> **#RebelMindset: Everyone, yes...everyone has a unique selling proposition. So, if you hate the question: "What makes you different?" This is the time to figure that out.**

Here are a few of the most common differentiators that organizations are known for. Which one is yours?

- Experience:
    - o Do you have team members who specialize in a rare industry skill?

- o Do your years of experience in your field outweigh a new college grad with a higher degree than yours?
- Niche Industry Knowledge:
  - o Focusing on industries with unique situations enables you to provide specialized solutions that maximize revenue and build stronger customer relationships.
  - o Understanding fully what the customer needs helps to reduce the sales cycle.
- Customer Service:
  - o Do you provide consistent follow-through and excellent results with minimal wait times and faster resolution of issues than your competition?
  - o Do you fulfill the promises you made during the sales process?
- Price: (tread lightly)
  - o Lowest cost can sometimes be perceived as low value as well.
  - o Highest cost: Does the customer see the value in paying more?
- Quality:
  - o Is your product or service consistently high quality so people are willing to pay more?
  - o Flip side: low cost and lower quality yet customers accept that and buy anyway.
- Value:
  - o Be creative with bundling products/services that add so much value that it's hard to say no.
  - o The bigger the problem, the more people are willing to spend to get rid of it!
- Solution-Based:
  - o Do you solve a problem faster, easier, and more effectively than your competitors?
  - o Is the product/service readily available vs. having to wait?
- Innovation:
  - o Continuous improvement on how your work gets done.

- o Coming up with faster and better results helps keep existing customers.
- Ease of Use:
  - o This can easily be related to value...the value of time. If you are easy to work with, convenient, and quickly solve the customers' problem(s), then the price is less of a factor.
  - o People will pay more for something that is easier to use and understand.

Your turn. Use the end of the chapter notes section or your Chapter 3 worksheet and write down what you want to be known for and why. Not sure? This is another great opportunity for you to engage your team and ask them what they think.

As you consider how you differentiate yourself from the competition, consider writing a USP: unique selling proposition. There are three do's and three don'ts associated with creating your unique selling proposition statement.

DO:
1. Use plain language. Speak as if you are at that 12th-grade Career Day.
2. Be specific. What about you and your services set you apart from your competition?
3. It's about them. Use customer-facing language that will resonate with them.

DON'T:
1. Slam your competition. It's bad form and you will sound petty.
2. Boast. It's not about you...it's about how you help your customers.
3. Ramble. Be brief about how you are unique; people will get lost in long explanations.

You are creating a succinct, one-sentence description of who you are, your biggest strength, and the major advantage that your customers will benefit from.

Here are a couple of national brand leaders' propositions:

- "*Sophisticated design at extremely low price*" IKEA®
- "*Empowering the world to design*" Canva®

> **#RebelMindset: If you could say anything about your organization without fear of judgment by others, what would you say? (This is where you tell your personal Tina to go take a nap!)**

Pricing Points to Ponder

Now that you understand what you sell and what makes you different, it's time to look at the basis of pricing. This section is overarching and not specific to any industry. We are simply looking to make sure we have a baseline understanding of how products and services could be priced.

This is a tricky topic and there are books JUST on how to price your product or service. For the purpose of this book, we are simply going to look at pricing from the 50,000-foot level to get a starting point of how pricing relates to your marketing.

When pricing a physical product, there are any number of costs, such as production costs, research and development, supply chain, staffing, buildings, maintenance, etc., to consider. It also takes an understanding of profit margins, markups, taxes, and the like when calculating a price. There are business coaches that specialize in the operations and financial aspects of manufacturing or wholesale business. I am not one of them. If you need a recommendation, let me know! I am happy to steer you in the right direction.

Most of my experience is in the B2B realm and with service-based industries. When pricing services, it comes down to the perceived value of that service to your customers. There are several questions you need to ask yourself when determining your pricing:

- How does your level of experience differentiate you?
- Do you fully understand how to resolve the problem?

- How effective is your solution?
- Will the outcome be a short-term or long-term solution?
- Does your solution increase productivity or increase the customer's revenue stream?

#RebelMindset: If you are giving them the answer to the test...you are worth more.

I had no idea how to price my marketing consulting services when I first started my business. None! I started by charging a fairly low hourly rate my first year and increased my fees as I gained more confidence in being a solopreneur. However, I knew I was still not charging enough when a customer said to me, "For what I learned from you and how you helped overhaul our marketing, I would have paid twice as much for your services." OUCH!

That comment made me take a long, hard look at what services I was offering customers. Then I consulted my mastermind group for some honest, shark-like, @$$-kicking advice. They helped me remove Tina from my head and allowed me to see the value I offer customers. It was life-changing!

I decided to narrow my services to marketing strategy vs day-to-day marketing design and implementation. Then, I moved to value-based pricing vs hourly fees. To move to value-based pricing, here is what I needed to understand:

- Just because it is easy for me, doesn't mean it is easy for my customers, so my services have a greater value.
- Experience and expertise add value; therefore, my services have a higher price point.
- If they could do it, they would not need me; I add value to their business.

Now, go back and read those last three bullet points with <u>you</u> as the subject matter expert. Do you still feel your services are priced properly? Or do you need a raise?

Common Pricing Strategies

As you read the following pricing strategies, I can almost guarantee you'll think of a time when these strategies have been applied to something you have bought. Which one makes the most sense for what you sell?

- **Competition-based pricing:** evaluating the prices set by your competitors, then setting it just above or below that price, depending upon what you are selling.
- **Cost-plus pricing:** this method is solely based on the cost of producing your product and then adding a markup so that you don't sell at a loss.
- **Economy pricing:** set the price to target buyers who seek a low price or bargain.
- **Premium pricing:** or "luxury" pricing. This is for products or services with proven quality and reliability.
- **Price skimming:** setting a high price for your product and then gradually reducing the price over time.
- **Value-based pricing:** targets a niche market with a product/ service that is customer-oriented and customizable according to the customer's needs; the higher the perceived value, the higher the price.

Do you currently use any of these strategies? This is not an exhaustive list and won't apply to anything and everything you can sell.

The bottom line: If pricing is a win/win for you (you make a profit) and the customer (they acquired value), then you have achieved an ethical pricing model. By doing this, customers will return, and they will send others your way.

#RebelMindset: If you made a bunch of money and the customer does not see the value, the backlash (especially with social media) is a long, hard recovery. Choose wisely!

Here is another way of looking at pricing from the one and only Warren Buffett: *"Price is what you pay. Value is what you get."*

Review Your RebelMindset

- Do you sell a product, service, or both?
- Differentiators set you apart and increase brand awareness.
- Price is a matter of perceived value: quality and/or convenience.

Chapter 3 Worksheet:

What do you sell:

☐ Service(s)

☐ Product(s)

☐ Both

What is your overarching category of what you sell?

(For example: consulting, supplier, contractor, accounting, nursing, mechanic, engineering, professional services, education, not-for-profit, etc.)

What specifically do you sell? Subcategory

(For example: **marketing** consulting, **industrial parts** supplier, **tax** accounting, **oncology** nursing, **large engine** mechanic, **legal** professional services, **higher** education, **children's** not-for-profit, etc.)

How would you answer these questions if you were talking to a 12th-grade class on Career Day?

1. What problems does your product/service solve for your customers?
2. What emotions are tied to solving the problems?
3. What features does it have to meet these needs?
4. What are the benefits of those features?
5. Where can the customer buy your product or service?
6. How and where will the customer use it?
7. How is it different from products/services by your competitors?

Circle which emotion(s) are tied to what you sell:

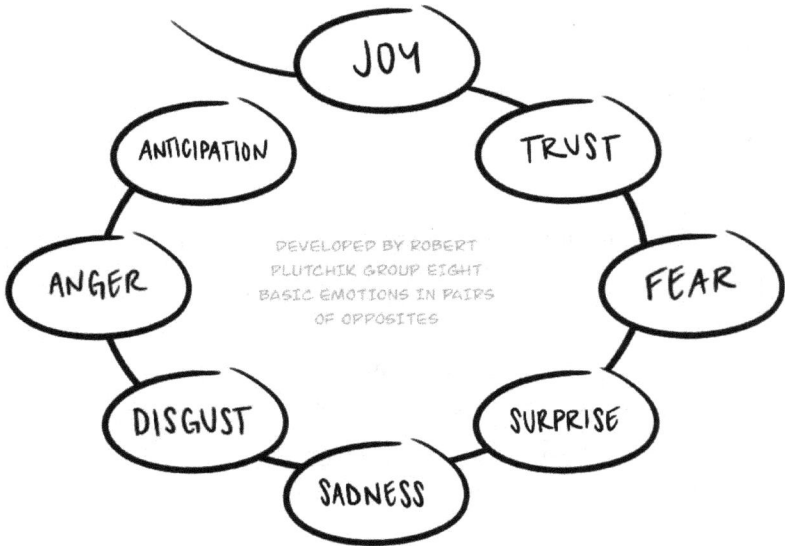

DEVELOPED BY ROBERT
PLUTCHIK GROUP EIGHT
BASIC EMOTIONS IN PAIRS
OF OPPOSITES

JOY

TRUST

FEAR

SURPRISE

SADNESS

DISGUST

ANGER

ANTICIPATION

Why did you circle that emotion?

What sets you apart from your competitors?

- Experience:
- Niche Industry Knowledge
- Customer Service (be specific)

- Price: (tread lightly)
- Quality
- Value
- Solution-Based
- Innovation
- Ease of Use

Unique Selling Proposition: Start the process by jotting down some notes about what you'd like your USP to say about you and your organization.

Here are some steps you can take to create your brand's proposition:

Step 1: Write down one or two characteristics of your target audience.

Step 2: Next, write down one or two problems you solve for your customers.

Step 3: What is unique about you or your organization?

Step 4: Clearly identify the promise you make to your customers.

Step 5: Create one paragraph that brings it all together.

Step 6: Shorten it to one sentence.

What pricing strategy do you use now? Is it working for you?

☐ Competition-based pricing

☐ Cost-plus pricing

☐ Economy pricing

☐ Premium pricing

☐ Price skimming

☐ Value-based pricing

CHAPTER 4

Ideal Customer vs. Target Audience: Know the Difference!

"When you speak to everyone, you speak to no one."
—MEREDITH HILL

My husband bought me a sweatshirt that says, "I am not responsible for what my face does when you talk!" He loves to say that he can have an entire conversation with me, and I don't have to say a word, he just needs to read my expressions. I need to control that better when business owners tell me, "Anyone can be my customer" while we are in the middle of a strategy session. I am sure my face does something weird based on their reactions. (TMI?)

Before we get too far into this topic, if you are using the PDF worksheets, head to rebelgirlmarketing.com/guide to print out the worksheet. Now back to our regularly scheduled program...

There is a distinct difference between your ideal customer and a target audience. Both are groups of people you want to get in front of; however, the messaging can be quite different.

Ideal customer: The person or organization you specifically want to work with or to buy your product/service. They have the budget, authority, need, and timing to buy what you sell. They fit the demographics and psychographics you establish. (Don't worry, we'll be discussing demo-and psychographics in a minute.)

Target audience: Where you find a grouping of ideal customers... simply put, it's where your ideal customer(s) hang out.

Within your target audience, you will find three sets of people:

- Buyers: the ones cutting the check
  o Think: the person whose reputation is on the line if you don't do your job well
- End users: the people using your product or service
  o Think: the person who is experiencing your product or service firsthand
- Influencers: the people who have influential power over the buyer
  o Think: someone who can sway the end user or buyer by their recommendation

> **#RebelMindset: A common influencer example is a four-year-old throwing a temper tantrum in the grocery store if they don't get the sugary cereal advertised during their cartoon hour. They are the influencer to the buyer and the end user. However, I don't recommend pitching a fit on the office floor to get your point across.**

Every day we see advertising for products that we don't buy, yet someone within our demographic or psychographic does, indicating we are in that brand's target audience.

For example, you are not currently in the market to buy a vehicle, even though you are constantly seeing advertisements for cars, trucks, SUVs, minivans, and the like. You may not be the buyer, but still, you could be the end user and/or influencer. For the vehicle manufacturer's marketing, it is very likely that one day, you will be the buyer, so they play the long game and hope when your need for a new vehicle arises, you remember their brand and products.

Identifying Your Ideal Customer – Demographics

Demographics are the measurable identifiers and statistical characteristics of a population, all the details about us that can be measured. Common demographics include, yet are not limited to:

- Age
- Gender
- Ethnicity
- Income
- Homeowner/renter
- Marital status
- Geographic location
- Number of children
- Vehicle type
- Occupation
- Education level

There are any number of demographics you can track based on what you sell, whether you are B2B or B2C.

Identifying Your Ideal Customer – Psychographics

Psychographics are the intangible characteristics of your ideal customer. It is known as the study of personality, values, opinions, attitudes, interests, and lifestyles. Common psychographics include:

- Beliefs and opinions
- Aspirations, goals, dreams, and wishes
- Interests
  - (pets, travel, wealth building)
- Activities
  - (hobbies, books, movies, charitable work)
- Personality and values
- Lifestyle and priorities
- How they spend their money
- Worries and fears

It's important to note that people with the same demographics do not always have the same psychographics and vice versa. Your product/service solves a problem and fills a need for your customers, so base the identifying characteristics of your ideal customer on the problem(s) you solve if you don't have past customers to pull from. Ask yourself, "Who needs what I sell?"

Knowing both the demographic and psychographic characteristics of your ideal customer allows you to provide a more personalized customer experience, which leads to higher engagement with your marketing efforts and, therefore, increased brand loyalty. How do you determine these characteristics? Start with thinking of the best customers you have ever had. What made them different from the other customers?

Let me give you an example of my ideal customer for Rebel Girl Marketing, LLC:

Demographics:

- *Occupation*: solo entrepreneur or small business owner with no dedicated sales or marketing roles

Psychographics:

- *Beliefs and opinions*: marketing is a necessary part of doing business
- *Aspirations, goals, dreams, and wishes*: growing their business
- *Values and personality*: understands hard work, willing to learn from me, and willing to roll up their sleeves to figure out the best way to move their business forward.
- *Personality*: no asshats; they put their ego aside and open their mind.
- *Lifestyle and priorities*: wants a better work/life balance by attracting the right customers and is not in it only for the money
- *How they spend their money*: willing to part with monies that make sense, no penny pinchers
- *Worries and fears:* afraid they will lose their business if they don't make a change

As you can see from my ideal customer profile, psychographics has a LOT more to do with whom I am targeting. Age, gender, geographic region, housing, vehicle, etc. have no bearing on whether they would be a good customer or not. What matters to me is their mindset on marketing, their willingness to be coached, and their motivation to do the work that needs to be done.

For you and your industry, the tables may be turned, and demographics are a critical part of whom you have as a customer. This is an important step in your marketing strategy, so take some time and really think about what makes up your ideal customer.

Now, it's your turn. Take out your worksheet for this chapter and list as many of the demo and psychographics you can think of for your ideal customer. To help you picture your ideal customer, create an avatar like the one I have below. There is a blank one on your worksheet and at the back of this chapter for you to complete. To the best of your knowledge, write down what you think are the characteristics of your ideal customer as well as what characteristics you are going to avoid like a crocodile with a toothache.

> **#RebelMindset: Your ideal customer can change based on how your business evolves, changes in the economy, technology, how people consume what you sell, or any other number of reasons. Be sure to reevaluate the definition of your ideal customer on a regular basis.**

Go to the back of this chapter or your worksheet and jot down five people or organizations you currently work with that fit your ideal customer profile. While you are there, think of five people or organizations that fit this profile that you want to target as prospects. You may want to dog-ear that page so as you think of more people/organizations to target, you know where to jot them down.

Target Audience

Now that you know whom you want to talk to, let's discover where they hang out, both digitally and physically.

The best place to start is by thinking of where you found your existing customers.

- Did you meet them at an event? Networking/Conference?
- Was it a referral?
- Are they a repeat customer? (also known as a boomerang customer, and it's more fun to say)
- Did they find you online?

Below is the list of marketing channels from Chapter 1 with examples for where both B2C and B2B customers could be found. Remember, this is not an exhaustive list and there are any number of other channels to choose from, so use your worksheet to customize your customer's "hang out" locations.

- **Direct selling:** in-person conversations
  - B2C: retail, ecommerce

- o B2B: 1:1 conversation for customized products like professional services (legal, accounting, insurance, marketing consulting) or high-ticket items like manufacturing or construction
- **Catalog direct:** you get these in the mail or pick up at a retail location
  - o B2C: holiday items, stationery, clothing
  - o B2B: office supplies, warehouse needs, industry apparel, promotional items
- **Social media:** as of 2022, there are now over 130 types of social media, YIKES!!
  - o B2C: anything really, the key is to know which ones your audience uses
  - o B2B: this will depend upon the product that you sell, i.e., professional services would be geared toward a LinkedIn strategy, where professional photography (being a visual product/service) would benefit from Pinterest or Instagram.
- **Digital advertisements:** think pop-up advertising
  - o B2C: ecommerce sites, regional retail/restaurants, sales events
  - o B2B: ecommerce, job postings, nationwide brands
- **Events:** in-person gatherings of like minded people to sell to and/or inform
  - o B2C: home parties, farmer's markets, home & garden shows
  - o B2B: industry conferences, trade shows
- **SEO marketing:** using key words and phrases typed into search engines
  - o B2C: everyone
  - o B2B: everyone
- **Email marketing:** they come into your email inbox, (duh)
  - o B2C: ecommerce, targeted regional audience for retail locations, sales events
  - o B2B: newsletters, blogs, sales events for existing customers, industry events

- **Direct mail:** arrives in your mailbox at work or at home
  - B2C: household services (lawncare, painting, cleaning), banking, dare I say it... political campaigns
  - B2B: printing services, professional cleaning services, banking, event invitations
- **Networking:** virtual or in-person events intended for meeting others
  - B2C: BNI is popular amongst both B2C and B2B, chambers of commerce, industry groups
  - B2B: chambers of commerce, industry groups (both your industry and the industries you sell to), social groups, educational organizations, entrepreneur groups

It is overwhelming, I get it! Don't forget to breathe...count of five breathe in...count of five breathe out...and repeat.

To add to the confusion, each of these channels has a strategy of its own! This chapter is intended for you to think about the places your ideal customers are and then determine which channel(s) you are willing to spend your time and money on.

> **#RebelMindset: Pick two and do them very, very well. You cannot be everywhere all the time.**

Go back to the Chapter 1 worksheet and look at what you wrote for current use and possible future use. Do you still feel like your answers are accurate? Circle one: YES / NO If your answer is NO, then use the table at the back of this chapter to mark where your target audience hangs out. Then, circle the two you want to focus on.

Within each of these channels you will find your buyers, end-users, and influencers. Take a look at your past and existing customer list. Find the customers that you wish you could clone, figure out where you found them, and start there. If you want to dive into the deep end of the pool and focus on one or two channels, you can find training or a book on how to best create strategies for that specific marketing channel or hire a professional. You can also take an online learning class like Udemy or LinkedIn Learning.

Knowing whom you need to talk to and where they hang out is crucial to making sure your marketing strategy (and budget) is reaching the right audience.

Review Your RebelMindset

- Demographics: tangible characteristics
- Psychographics: intangible characteristics
- Channels: where does your ideal customer hang out?
  - o Pick two channels to use and do them very, very well!

Chapter 4 Worksheet:

Demographics and psychographics: Fill in each section that applies to your ideal customer. If you don't know, circle the category and make a note to research that category.

AGE

GENDER

ETHNICITY

INCOME

HOMEOWNER/RENTER

MARITAL STATUS

GEOGRAPHICAL LOCATION

NUMBER OF CHILDREN

VEHICLE TYPE

OCCUPATION

EDUCATION LEVEL

OTHER

DEMOGRAPHICS VS. PSYCHOGRAPHICS

BELIEFS AND OPINIONS

ASPIRATIONS AND DREAMS

INTERESTS

ACTIVITIES

PERSONALITY AND VALUES

LIFESTYLE AND PRIORITIES

HOW THEY SPEND THEIR MONEY

WORRIES AND FEARS

OTHER

Ideal Customers

Current Customers	Potential Customers
1.	1.
2.	2.
3.	3.
4.	4.
5.	5.

Channel	Use Now?	Use in Future?	Learn or outsource?
Catalog			
Digital advertisements			
Direct mail			
Direct selling			
Email marketing			
Events			
Networking			
Search Engine Optimization (SEO)			
Other:			

CHAPTER 5

Quit Sounding Like Everyone Else

"Marketing is no longer about the stuff that you make, but about the stories you tell."
—SETH GODIN

> **#RebelMindset: Marketing is storytelling and selling is simply telling that story to others.**

Most people hate networking events for two main reasons:

1. They feel like they are constantly being sold to.
2. They have no idea what to say.

In this chapter, you won't be creating a simple elevator pitch, you will be creating a Power Pitch! When you know exactly what to say to your audience, creating marketing content, networking, and selling is a lot easier...and a lot more fun!

Before we go too much farther, please go to the back of this chapter or take out your Chapter 5 worksheet and complete exercise #1. You'll find the worksheet for this chapter at rebelgirlmarketing.com/guide.

I'm not kidding. It is helpful to have a baseline understanding of what you say now as your elevator pitch, so please complete

Exercise #1, it will only take a minute or so. Don't make me use my Mom voice…

Go ahead…I'll wait here.

Welcome back!

Most people think of an elevator pitch as telling the audience what you do in 30 seconds, or maybe two minutes. Or people see it as a sales pitch, otherwise known as the "let me prove why you should hire me in 30 seconds or less" pitch.

> **#RebelMindset. Instead of thinking of it as an elevator pitch, think of it as your first impression.**

I'll let that sink in for a minute: Your elevator pitch is your first impression. That being the case, let's get rid of elevator pitches and create a Power Pitch!

Before we get started, let's talk about four kinds of pitches we are going to avoid.

- "I'M JUST A…": This pitch is where you downplay your role. If you use these words, get rid of them! We destroyed those words in the introduction, so there is no place for them here either. You don't hear a CEO walking around saying, "I'm just the CEO." Their job is no more important than yours! You contribute. You work hard. You are an integral part of your department. You are not allowed to say, "I'm just a" ever again because that's not true.

- SHOW-UP&THROW-UP: The next type of pitch we're going to avoid is the *show-up and throw-up*. What does that mean? When you ask someone, "So what do you do?" That person keeps talking… and talking…and talking. By the end, you know what they're doing that weekend, the names of their kids and their pets, where they went to school, all of the places that they've ever worked in their entire lifetime, and even more! (You are thinking of someone right now who does that aren't you? Or is it you?)

- WORD PULLING: This next one is the opposite of the show-up and throw-up, I call it *word pulling* because this is the person who doesn't give you any information at all. Let me give you an example.

You ask, "So what do you do?"

The person replies, "I'm in sales."

So, then you ask, "Whom do you work for?"

They reply, "ABC Company."

You ask, "What do you sell?"

And they reply with yet another 10-syllable or less answer.

What do you do with so little information?!

- SUBJECT MATTER EXPERT: The last pitch to avoid I call the *subject matter expert pitch*. That's a pitch that is very high level or conversely, incredibly detailed, using tons of acronyms and industry jargon that when the person is done talking, you still have NO idea what they do. Let me put it this way, if the other person understood this kind of pitch, they probably don't need your services.

None of these pitches make a great first impression. I know this because at some point in my career, I have done them ALL!

Power Pitch Defined

Now that we are done with the "don't" list, let's talk about what makes a great Power Pitch.

- 15 seconds: A Power Pitch is 8.25 seconds or less. Why? Because the average human has an eight-second attention span[1]. Yep. Eight seconds. All you need to do in those first 15 seconds is to capture their attention and get them to start asking questions.
- Conversation starter: Aside from being your first impression, think of your pitch like a baseball game. The game doesn't start until somebody throws out the first pitch. In a networking situation,

---

[1] https://www.thetreetop.com/statistics/average-human-attention-span#:~:text=Average%20Human%20Attention%20Span%20Statistics&text=The%20average%20human%20attention%20span,seconds%20to%20over%2020%20minutes.

your Power Pitch is simply used to start a conversation. If you are asked to give a 30- or 60-second pitch, then start with your Power Pitch to gain the audience's attention, then talk about one of the problems you solve to fill the rest of the time. Or, better yet…tell a story of how you solved a problem for a customer.

- <u>Show value</u>: A Power Pitch tells how you add value to your customers' lives, how you make their lives easier, and the problems you solve for them.

Storytime! When I did this training for a young entrepreneurs' group, I had one of the participants give me his old pitch, which went something like this: *Hi, my name is John. I'm a handyman. I clean gutters and sometimes I have to fix the gutters and sometimes I fix the shingles while I'm up there too. But I don't do a lot of electrical, I don't like electrical but then I do some plumbing and I've done some landscaping, but you know I've done dry walling and painting and…*(I'll stop there – this is an example of a Show-Up & Throw-Up pitch.) It was a bit reminiscent of that scene in the movie *Forrest Gump* and the bus ride with Bubba, and how Bubba was telling Forrest all the different ways you can make shrimp.

After John went through the Power Pitch exercise, he came up with this pitch: *Hi, my name is John, and I am a handyman. I do all of the things on your home to-do list that you hate to do.* Short and shows how he improves the lives of his customers. And, I can almost guarantee you thought of a thing or two on your home to-do list you want John to do!

- <u>Your WHY</u>: A Power Pitch can also contain your "WHY." If you are a Simon Sinek fan like me, you have read his books *Start with WHY* and/or *Find Your WHY*. If not, then let me kindly suggest you take five minutes and scan the QR code next to this section and watch Simon's Ted Talk from 2016 that talks about "The Golden Circle." Developing your WHY is not something you come up with in a few minutes. It takes acting like a three-year-old and keep asking yourself "why?" until you come to the core reason of what you do and why you do it.

Another **Storytime**! When I presented this topic to a different group of entrepreneurs and I came to this part of the training, one participant raised her hand and proclaimed that she doesn't have a "WHY." I of course said, "Yes, you do, come on up!" She came to the front of the room, and I asked her, "Why did you start your business?" She said, "It's great money." Money is a motivator, it's not your why. Let me repeat that, money is a motivator…it's not your why. Then she said, "There's nothing like it in the area." I said, "Perfect. That is great for your business plan, but it's still not your WHY." I continued to ask her why she started her business a few more times until we finally discovered her "WHY." She said, "When women walk into my hair salon, they're walking in at a normal pace, not really any kind of expression on their face, shoulders are down. But when they walk out of my salon, their head is high, their shoulders are back, they've got a smile on their face, and they look like they're ready to take on their world." Confidence. She doesn't sell hairstyles, she sells confidence. That is a great WHY.

Creating Your Power Pitch

This may take you a little bit of time. However, it is very important that you complete all five questions before you try to create a new pitch.

📄 You will need your worksheet or turn to the back of this chapter to complete this exercise. Take your time and fill in these questions to the best of your ability.

1. <u>What do you do</u>? This can simply be your title or a brief description of your role.
2. <u>How do you do your job</u>? What are the day-to-day activities you conduct to do your job? You don't need to write down every single

activity, just the overarching action items like, one-to-one meetings with your team, set up customer appointments, design blueprints, create proposals, input on Excel spreadsheets, write reports, answer customer questions…you get the idea.

3. <u>What problems do you solve?</u> Whatever you do, you're solving a problem. For example, a problem any restaurant's wait staffs solves is they bring food to hungry people. A sales person brings in revenue for the company by solving their customer's problems. A physical therapist helps their patients relieve pain or strengthen certain parts of the body. In each of these examples, a problem was solved simply by doing their job. What problems do you solve?

4. <u>What emotions are tied to solving those problems?</u> What emotions do you feel when you solve a customer's problem and/or what emotions do your customers feel when their problem is solved? For example, I have a friend who is a life coach. She uses these words to describe how her customers feel when working with her: people feel safe, they have hope, feel joy, feel fulfillment, and have an increase inself-worth. These are all the emotions that are attached to the problems that she solves.

   a. To help you with this question, here is Robert Plutchik's wheel of emotion that includes the eight baseline emotions we all have, just like we discussed in Chapter 3. Feel free to refer back to the Chapter 3 worksheet for the answers to this question.

5. <u>Your WHY</u>: As I mentioned before, I am a bit of a Simon Sinek fan. This section is based on his concept of the Golden Circle. (if you didn't watch the video, now is a good time to do so.) Your why is about why you are in business in the first place. Why did you pick the industry that you're in? Everybody has a WHY. Let me tell you the story of Daniel. Daniel owns a roofing company. When I asked him why he is in the roofing industry, he said the same thing lots of people say, "Good money." He also answered, "It's what I've done all my life." You know me well enough by now to know that I did not let him off the hook until we got to his real WHY. What we uncovered is, that by doing his job, he keeps people safe. That's the problem he solves and that's a great WHY! Again…it's not about the money.

📄 Exercise #2: By answering the questions first, the next section will have a greater impact on creating your Power Pitch.

Power Words

Once you're done filling in those five questions, I'd like you to go back to each section and circle some Power Words. Power Words are the words that are going to resonate best with the people you're talking to, not the words that you like. Back in Chapter 4 we talked about whom your ideal customer is…picture those people as you circle your power words.

> **#RebelMindset: It's not about what you want them to hear. It's about how you tell your story in a way they can understand.**

Pitching Lesson

Using the Power Words you circled, let's create your Power Pitch. The most important part of having a pitch is it needs to sound like you. If you swear, and your audience is okay with it, then put a swear word in there if you'd like. My friend Susie is a part-time operations manager for small businesses. Her pitch is, "I get sh!t done." She's the behind-the-scenes person who gets everything done for her customers so they can do what they do best. The key is to know your audience.

Exercise #3: Now it's your turn. To get started, below you will find three different approaches to saying your Power Pitch. These are simply to get you thinking about how you can create your Power Pitch.

1. My job is to _____, so that _____
2. I support my customers by _____, so that they can _____
3. When you need _____, my job is to _____

> **#RebelMindset: Use these only as a starting point. The more you use your Power Pitch, the more you will refine it to sound like you.**

As an example, here is my Power Pitch:

"As a marketing strategist, it is my job to make sure that when your customers and prospects need what you sell, they think of you first."

I did not use the word consultant; I used strategist, which tells them I specialize. I talked about their customers and prospects, so they picture them and then hit them with solving the problem of brand awareness by mentioning being thought of first when needs arise. This is a pitch I use when talking to business owners or executives. This Power Pitch is less than 15 seconds and tells the audience how I add value.

In a general networking situation, I use a Power Pitch that is less than 15 seconds and tells them my WHY. It goes like this:

"I create marketing strategies that help small businesses stay in business."

As a reminder, the point of a Power Pitch is to get the person you are talking to in engage in the conversation and ask questions. As long as they are asking questions, they are absorbing the information and are much more likely to remember you and your conversation.

If you need to include your name and company name, then say that last. People tend to remember the last thing they heard better than the first thing.

"If you can't explain it simply, you don't know it well enough." – Albert Einstein

Stun Them, Don't Stumble

Just like in a baseball game, the pitcher doesn't show up five minutes before the game starts. What does he do? Yep, practice, practice, practice.

It is important to practice your pitch because the last thing you want to do when somebody asks is stare into space and say, "Oh, gee, I know this one. Hold on. Just give me a second. I even read this book and wrote it down…"

You want to say your Power Pitch immediately. Knowing exactly what to say and how to say it creates a great first impression!

The best way to practice is to record yourself, audio and video. Why video? Well, depending upon which study you look at, 70 to 90 percent of your message is conveyed through *nonverbal* communication. Video is the best way to see what your face is doing as well as your gestures. If you're anything like me, you talk with your hands. Sometimes I get so animated when I talk, my arms flail about and it looks like I'm trying to land a plane! This is why *seeing* how you look when you say your pitch is important.

You could also practice in front of a mirror, and you must say it out loud. Pace, tone, speed, and inflections all contribute to how the other person interprets your words.

#RebelMindset: What you say silently in your head usually sounds completely different than when you say it out loud. It's okay to talk to yourself, or the cat/dog/hamster/fish/mailbox...

The best way to practice is to say your Power Pitch in front of a friend, coworker, or somebody in your networking group. Practice with someone who knows you well and is going to be honest with you. You want that person to be trustworthy to tell you if your pitch is working or not.

So, practice, practice, practice.

Power Words Put to Good Use

You wrote down a ton of words during this chapter. You can use them to create other content for your marketing like:

- tagline
- closing statement for blogs and in articles
- social posts
- website
- mission or power statement

Create content that your audience understands and don't forget to have fun, use some casual words, and most importantly...be yourself!

In Chapter 3 we worked on your Unique Selling Proposition (USP). Now that you have your Power Words, go back and reread your USP. Would any of your power words work in that statement?

You're Not Alone

Your Power Pitch is going to help you set the tone for that first impression. Think about how much more fun networking is going to be now that you have the confidence of knowing exactly what you want to say. In Chapter 10 we will be talking about Networking on Purpose, knowing where to go to reach your target audience.

In the meantime, enlist the support of the people around you to create a Power Pitch and marketing content that grabs and keeps the attention of your audience. Remember, marketing is a team sport!

#RebelMindset: What is your team saying about your brand when they are out networking? Walk through this chapter with your team so your brand message is consistent and accurate.

Review Your RebelMindset

- Your Power Pitch is less than 15 seconds, shows how you add value, or tells your WHY.
- Use words that your audience will connect with.
- Practice to be professional.

Chapter 5 Worksheet:

Exercise #1: Take out your phone and go to the stopwatch feature. Pretend you are at a networking event, and someone asks you the question, "So, what do you do?'"

- Say your elevator pitch (OUT LOUD) and record how long it takes you to say it.
- Current elevator pitch time: _____ seconds

Exercise #2: Building your elevator pitch

WHAT do you do? (i.e.: your title):

HOW do you do your job?

What problem(s) do you solve for your customers/customers?

How do they (or you) feel once you have solve their problem(s)?

This is WHY I do it:

Exercise #3: Pulling It All Together

1. My job is to _____

    _____, so that _____

    _____

2. I support my customers by _____

    _____, so that they can _____

    _____

3. When you need _____

    _____, my job is to _____

    _____

4. Use your own words:

Now… Read your new pitch… what is your new time? _____
seconds

PART 2

Taking Your Marketing Knowledge to the Next Level

CHAPTER 6

Everything Is Marketing! Yes, Everything

"Content marketing is really like a first date. If all you do is talk about yourself, there won't be a second date."
—DAVID BEEBE

Marketing Geeks Unite!

Yes, I know I'm the marketing geek, yet stay with me here. Think about everything that you do on a day-to-day basis as you go about your business. Remember, marketing is perception; therefore, everything you do in a day that has to do with your business is being perceived by others.

Still don't believe me? Consider the following:

- How do you pull into the parking lot? Are you cautious or is it like you're finishing the race for the Indy 500?
- How do you walk into the building? Do you just go straight to your office and close the door or do you say hello along the way?
- What does your voice mail greeting sound like? Does it say things like, "Hey I'm so glad you called I can't wait to get back to you." or does it have that tone of, "I'm just too busy to answer your question and I may or may not call you back."
- Are you on time for meetings or chronically late?

- Do you answer your phone during meetings or when you're out networking? This signifies that whoever is on the phone is more important than the person right in front of you.
- Do your invoices say, "Thank you for doing business with us?"
- Do your proposals say, "I look forward to working with you?"
- What about your physical space? When you're on a Zoom call, look behind you. I can't tell you how many times I've seen dirty laundry or dishes behind someone on a virtual call. Your background doesn't have to be interior-designer-perfect; it just needs to look professional.
- Speaking of physical space, if you have a retail shop or office that customers come to, what's the general vibe people get when they walk in? Remember the five senses in Chapter 1? How does it smell? Is it warm? Is it cold? All of those things are going to matter when it comes to your physical space.

I'll stop there.

Before we go any further, be sure to find the questions at the end of this chapter or print out the PDF worksheet for Chapter 6 at rebelgirlmarketing.com/ guide You can start by answering the questions listed above.

These are just a few examples of how your day-to-day actions can influence perceptions. As you go through your day, be mindful of how your customers and team members are perceiving you, your team, your brand, and the overall experience with your organization.

Perception can be fickle. As the one-and-only Warren Buffet said, "*It takes 20 years to build a reputation and five minutes to ruin it. If you think about that, you'll do things differently.*"

The Story Is Yours…The Journey Is Theirs…

Yes, the story you are telling in your marketing is about you and your organization. And, yes, the story you are telling is about how you solve the customers' problems with your products/services. However, the *journey* is your customers'!

Let me say that again, *the story is yours…the journey is theirs.*

The Customers' Journey

Your customers' journey is each and all interactions customers have with you, your product/service, your team, and your environment. The journey starts before the customer knows you exist and ends with your final communication with that customer. And, just like any journey…there needs to be a strategy for getting from Point A to Point B, and a reward at the end of the journey.

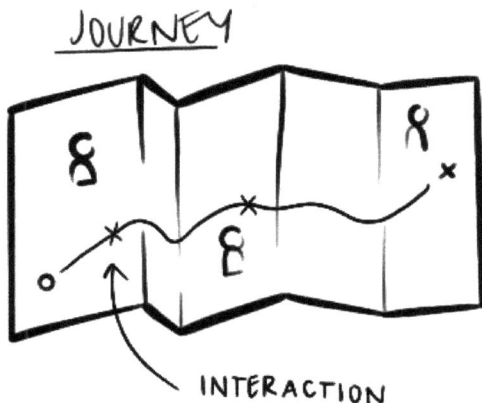

#RebelMindset: Going forward in this book, we are going to make a shift in thinking. From here on out, put yourself in the customers' seat and view your marketing and sales efforts from their perspective.

Look at your notes from Chapter 4 and read through the list of attributes that make up your ideal customer. If it helps, you can picture people you have worked with in the past. Personally, I picture two incredibly different people in my mind when developing my own marketing. I picture one customer that I LOOOOVE to work with. They are fun, eager to learn and implement ideas, have the best interest of their team and their customers in mind, and love what they do for a living. Then there is the other person, someone I did NOT enjoy working with. They were short-tempered, didn't want to do the work, were never wrong, and only thought of the bottom line (you only make the mistake of working with that kind of customer once!). Yet, they both motivate me to picture and seek out the right customer to work with and to create the right content for my marketing. If you are a visual person, you could do like my fellow-entrepreneur friend did. He created an actual picture that represents his ideal customer and put it on the wall behind his desk. Any time he is creating marketing or is prospecting, he looks at that picture to remind himself of whom he wants as a customer.

To create your customers' journey, let's bring back KNOW | LIKE | TRUST we learned about in Chapter 1.

KNOW (aka: brand awareness)

Customers need to know you exist before they can buy from you… obviously.

Ask yourself: "What is one of the first things I do when I need to research a topic or buy something?" More than likely, you pick up your phone or go to your laptop and look it up using a search engine. According to Forbes research,[1] around 93 percent of online experiences begin with a search engine. This is why your online presence is so very, very, very (yes, three verys for emphasis) important in your marketing. VERY! It does not matter if you are B2C or B2B, your online presence is the first place people go to KNOW about you.

If you still don't believe me, here are a few stats that will help you better understand my over-exaggeration with the word "very":

---

[1] https://www.forbes.com/sites/ajagrawal/2017/08/30/how-to-optimize-your-seo-results-through-content-creation/?sh=d231622aa37b

- 70 to 90 percent of a buying decision happens before a salesperson gets involved (Source: Gartner)[2]
- nine out of Ten B2B buyers say online content has a moderate to major effect on purchasing decisions (Source: CMO Council)[3]
- 84 percent of CEOs and VPs use social media to make purchasing decisions (Source: HBR[4] / IDC)
- 73 percent of B2B buyers say a web search was one of the first three resources they use to learn about a solution (Source: Marketing Charts)[5]

Let's take a pause here. Head to the back of this chapter or pull out your Chapter 6 PDF worksheet. Write down all of the places you can be found online. There are some categories already listed and blank spots for you to fill in other online locations.

On a scale from 1 to 4 (1 being "oh crap!" to 4 being "I'm a rockstar!") rate your online presence for each online channel in two categories: accuracy and consistency.

- Accuracy for how accurate and relevant the information is (logo, hours, address, phone number, products/services you offer, etc.... you get the point)
- Consistency for how often you update or post on that online channel

Go ahead. I'll wait here.

If you are closer to "oh crap!" than "I'm a rockstar!" for most of your online presence, that is the first thing you will want to take care of or have someone on your team do it. Soon. Think of it this way: If your potential customers are mostly driving in the "oh crap!" lane

---

[2] https://www.gartner.com/en/digital-markets/insights/saas-value-proposition

[3] https://www.cmocouncil.org/

[4] https://hbr.org/2019/03/the-best-ways-to-use-social-media-to-expand-your-network

[5] https://www.marketingcharts.com/industries/business-to-business-114754

at the beginning of their journey…chances are they will veer off that lane and head in the direction of your competitors.

There are many other ways potential customers can find out about you; it is not all done online. Utilizing advertising, sponsorships, speaking events, articles, networking, conferences, and expos are all good ways to expose your brand to your target audience.

> **#RebelMindset: The fastest way to get new clients is referrals or word-of-mouth marketing. This is when existing or past customers send people your way. And the best way to get referrals is to have an excellent customer journey! (See how I came full circle on that one?)**

LIKE (aka: content and personal experience)

Once someone knows you exist and they take that first step to interact with you, the LIKE process begins. However, as the quote in the beginning of this chapter alluded to, if everything is about you, people will be less likely to stick around. Your marketing is about how you solve your customers' problems. It needs to pique curiosity and give just enough information that the audience takes action to learn more.

Reviews are a large part of the LIKE process, especially in the B2C space. Think of the last time you were searching for a new restaurant. Aside from checking out the menu and pictures of the food, I can almost guarantee you also looked at the reviews before making a decision as to whether or not to try that restaurant. And if you find a bad review, yet the restaurant responded with helpful and caring words, does the bad review still negatively sway your decision to try that restaurant?

Now it's time to ask yourself, "Is my marketing more about me or my customers?"

Here is where the rubber meets the road on your customers' journey. Grab any piece of your marketing material you have handy. You can go to your website, social media, print ad, printed sales material, or even your business card. Read it as if you are the customer.

- Does it only try to sell them on your product or service, or does it inform?
- Does it show how you are a subject matter expert?
- Does it show how you solve problems?
- Does it have a call to action?

You are probably saying, "Stop! You ask so many questions, Lisa!!" I know… all I am trying to do is make you think differently and have the RebelMindset of seeing through your customers' eyes.

Here is the good news: Now that you are seeing things from the LIKE perspective, you can take content you have already created, tweak it so it reads from a customer's perspective, and reuse it. It's okay. Nobody is going to call you out on it, and it will save you lots of time and money vs creating all new content.

#RebelMindset: Marketing happens between KNOW and LIKE. Selling happens between LIKE and TRUST.

TRUST (aka: selling process)

Your potential customer KNOWs you exist, LIKEs what you have to say, and now is the time for building TRUST.

Before we talk about how to build trust, let's define it. The *Oxford English Dictionary* defines trust as *reliability, truth, ability, or strength.*

These four traits are what the customer is looking to gain from you:

- Customers *rely* on you to fulfill what was promised to them during the sales process.

- They trust you to tell the *truth* about cost, availability, quality, and the like.
- They need to know you will be there when they need you.
- The product/service needs to be as good as you promised, *strengthening* brand loyalty.

Bottom line: When someone trusts that you have these attributes, they will buy from you. When you fulfill their expectations, they will buy from you again.

B2C selling usually happens through ecommerce or in a brick-and-mortar store.

- Ecommerce is all about quick and easy sales. Information found online about the product needs to be accurate and informative. The better your technology and your SEO marketing, the easier and quicker someone can find and order your products. If it takes too long, you lose them. (Remember, the average person only has an eight-second attention span.)
- Brick-and-mortar store sales are about availability and customer service. Trust is built through interpersonal interactions, product knowledge, and answering questions.

Storytime! My husband and I were playing cards with another couple who are building a home. They were telling us the ups and downs of home building and the 400+ selections they needed to make, you know, tile, cabinets, cabinet handles, paint colors, and so on. Part of this process is selecting the appliances. Our friends went to three places to look for appliances that would fit within their design style, room dimensions, and budget.

As we learned earlier in this chapter, they had already completed over 70 percent of the buying process by researching the sizes, styles, and prices online. All they needed was to see the products in person and order what they wanted. Two of the appliance stores were friendly enough, yet not very knowledgeable about the different brands, and the entire time kept trying to upsell them to more expensive appliances. The third store's salesperson showed them the exact appliances they were looking for, gave them an estimated delivery date, and even offered to store the appliances in the store's warehouse if the appliances arrived before the house was finished. No upselling, just great service. The funny part was the pricing at the third store was more than at the first two. The salesperson at the third store gained their trust by providing knowledgeable information, excellent service with no upselling, and solving a possible problem before it even existed.

What does this one couple have to do with B2C marketing? Word of mouth! Our friends are telling that story to others, creating positive brand awareness for store #3 and negative awareness for stores #1 and #2. They also have a whole bunch of other items to purchase for the new house and guess where they will be heading back to? Yep, store #3.

> *"It takes months to find a customer... seconds to lose them."*
> —VINCE LOMBARDI

In most B2B selling, the sales process is much longer and takes place between the potential customer and a sales professional. Competition can be tough and sometimes it comes down to the relationship you build with the customer that wins the sale. Building the trust of the customer starts from their first interaction with your organization. How quickly do you respond to a sales inquiry? How informed is the sales professional? Are you selling only on price, or do you also bring value?

The best way to build and keep your customer's trust is to be prepared! Especially before that first sales conversation, do your homework on the person whom you are meeting with as well as on the organization they represent.

Without crossing the line of being a creepy stalker, you can search for the person on social media channels, particularly LinkedIn. Knowing someone's professional background and what they post or share on LinkedIn will give you a baseline understanding of their interests, education, and common connections. If you are meeting someone cold (as in you've never met them before, not their personality) and you have common connections on LinkedIn, it may be in your best interest to call your common connection and find out more about your potential customer.

Finding out what you can about the organization is also helpful, especially if you have specific demographics for the kinds of organizations you work with, such as industry, revenue or employee size, geographic reach, and so on.

Using phrases like, "According to the research I did on your organization…" and then listing what you found, will do two things: It will tell the person you are meeting with that you did your homework, and it will confirm the details you found online. You will find people are more open to you and your questions once they know you are prepared and ready to do business.

> **#RebelMindset: Walking into a sales meeting with a potential customer assuming you already know what they need before you have even had a conversation does not build trust.**

There are two basic roles you can play in any conversation: the adult (authoritative) or the child (inferior). Let me explain:

- If you walk into a sales call with the attitude that the potential customer is an idiot if they don't buy from you, it puts you in the authoritative position and your prospect in the inferior position. Don't do that…

- If you walk into a sales call praying, begging, and pleading with the potential customer to buy from you, it puts you in the inferior position and them in the authoritative position. Don't do that either…

- What you want is an adult-to-adult conversation where it is a mutually beneficial relationship, aka: you both win.

During your conversations with a customer, the very best way to build trust is by listening more than talking. Do either of these popular sayings sound familiar?

Listen to learn, not to respond.
You have two ears and one mouth, use them proportionately.

Asking targeted questions that get the potential customer to talk freely is a great way to uncover unknown needs and possibly sell more products/services than you anticipated.

Storytime! I have a customer who hired me to create an email campaign strategy that involved four different products/departments within the organization. Each department sent out their own emails. The problem was that too many emails were going out on the same day to the same email list and the four departments were not letting each other know what they were doing. This created numerous calls to customer service (making it five departments now involved) with customers asking to be taken off the email lists because emails were coming from multiple internal email addresses. The bigger problem of this issue was that email was the organization's main way of communicating with their customers. No emails = no sales.

I met with all five department heads, listened to their needs, and asked questions to gain a better understanding of what was truly happening behind the scenes. What I found was that the email problem that I was hired to fix was only a symptom of a larger

Stand up meetings *are short, productive meetings, that only discuss updates, wins, and stuck items for each person in the meeting. Stuck items are brainstormed right then and there. If a longer meeting is needed for stuck items, then a separate meeting is scheduled, and only key people are involved. This concept is taken from the book Traction by Gino Wickman discussing E.O.S. (Entrepreneurial Operating Systems)* problem. Each department had different ecommerce systems, different sales tracking systems, different email templates, and no consistent and coherent way of communicating with one another.

What started out as a month-long project to create email strategies ended up being a nine-month contract in which we revamped their entire customer journey for both external customers and internal ones (remember: internal marketing is all about communications with your team). We worked through internal communications first, creating a weekly stand-up meeting between departments, and biweekly department meetings with leadership. Then we assigned one person in the company to approve and schedule email campaigns using a new and redesigned email template that created consistency in their brand. We then combined ecommerce systems, sales tracking systems, launched a new website, and a new logo. It was awesome!

As a result of the strategies built along the way, their cyber-Monday sale did three times what it had done in the previous two years, incoming calls from prospective customers to their sales department went from three to five times a month to three times a week! Department leads reported better overall culture with their teams, and everyone started having fun again. The president said to me, "*I am finally proud of the marketing we put out to our customers.*"

All of this happened simply by asking questions, listening for cues of potential underlying problems, and providing solutions and strategies that benefited the entire organization. Your marketing and sales efforts are about the customer trusting you to fill the gap between what you promised and what you deliver.

#RebelMindset: Marketing is a mindset and everything you do and say has a direct relationship to how your brand is perceived by others. You don't need to walk on eggshells, just don't be an @$$hole.

Review Your RebelMindset

- Marketing is a mindset; it's in everything you do during your workday.
- Your online presence is your first impression with new customers.
- Listen to learn, not to respond.

Chapter 6 Worksheet:

- How do you pull into the parking lot? Are you cautious or is it like you're finishing the race for the Indy 500?
- How do you walk into the building? Do you just go straight to your office and close the door? Or do you say hello along the way?
- What does your voicemail greeting sound like? Does it say things like, "Hey, I'm so glad you called. I can't wait to get back to you." or does it have that tone of, "I'm just too busy to answer your question and I may or may not call you back." '
- Do your invoices say, "Thank you for doing business with us"?
- Do your proposals say, "I look forward to working with you"?
- Are you on time for meetings or chronically late?
- Do you answer your phone during meetings or when you're out networking? This signifies that whoever is on the phone is more important than the person right in front of you.
- What about your physical space? When you're on a Zoom call, please look behind you first. I can't tell you how many times I've seen dirty laundry or dishes behind someone on a virtual call. It doesn't have to be interior-design-perfect; it just needs to look professional.
- Speaking of physical space, if you have a retail shop or office that customers come into, what's the general vibe people get when they walk in? Remember the five senses in Chapter 1. How does it smell? Is it warm? Is it cold? All of those things are going to matter when it comes to your physical space.

Online Presence   1 = Oh Crap! 4 = I'm a Rock Star!

I can be found online here:	Accuracy				Consistency			
My website(s)	1	2	3	4	1	2	3	4
LinkedIn	1	2	3	4	1	2	3	4
Facebook	1	2	3	4	1	2	3	4
Instagram	1	2	3	4	1	2	3	4
Pinterest	1	2	3	4	1	2	3	4
Twitter	1	2	3	4	1	2	3	4
Industry Website(s)	1	2	3	4	1	2	3	4
Chamber of Commerce Website(s)	1	2	3	4	1	2	3	4
Google My Business	1	2	3	4	1	2	3	4
Yelp	1	2	3	4	1	2	3	4
	1	2	3	4	1	2	3	4
	1	2	3	4	1	2	3	4
	1	2	3	4	1	2	3	4
	1	2	3	4	1	2	3	4
	1	2	3	4	1	2	3	4

CHAPTER 7

Selling: It's Easier Than You Think

"Sales is not about selling anymore, but about building trust and educating."
—SIVA DEVAKI

You only need two things to be excellent at selling: a great story and the ability to listen. That's it!

Before I get into this chapter, I'd like to get on my soapbox and vent for a moment about how sales and marketing efforts need to work together. As a solo entrepreneur or small business owner, you may or may not have had the "pleasure" (term used loosely) of working in a corporate America setting where you had to deal with these two departments, so let me explain.

If I had a nickel for every time someone told me their sales and marketing departments didn't communicate on brand strategies, product launches, sales events, marketing campaigns, or anything related to business development as a whole...I'd be writing this book from my private island off Fiji!! It is sooooooooo frustrating to think that two departments that have the EXACT SAME goal of growing a business are working as if they are from different planets! UGH!

People! Get your heads out of your @$$ and talk to each other. You are ruining it for your team, your customers, your vendors, and your stakeholders.

Let me get you started. If you are in sales, go to the head of your marketing department and ask to sit in on marketing strategy meetings to see what ideas they are tossing around for future campaigns. If you are a marketing professional, go to your sales lead and ask to attend a few sales calls with both prospects and current customers.

Your job while with the other department is simply to listen to learn, not to respond. Then ask qualifying questions of the other department to make sure you understand what you've observed. Next, figure out how both departments can work better together going forward.

> **#RebelMindset: Remember, you are both on the same team...act like it!**

Okay, I'm done. Just give me a sec so I can step down off the soapbox and get to talking about selling for small businesses.

You'll be happy to know that there is not a lot of homework, so there is no worksheet for Chapter 7. For now, go to the end of this chapter and write down the people who handle the sales and/or marketing for your organization. Then jot down a couple of ideas for how they can work together in a more collaborative capacity.

Short Review

So far in this book, we have figured out why we need marketing, what we sell, whom we sell it to, where they hang out, what to say, and how everything you do has an effect on your business development efforts.

The lesson I would like you to take away from my outburst is that even though marketing and sales play different roles in helping to grow a business, they cannot do it without each other. As a small business owner, you need to keep that in mind as you develop your marketing strategies. Ask yourself who else needs to know about this within my own team? Better yet, ask the different departments to contribute to the brainstorming session you will be holding to create your marketing strategies.

For example, I was working with a manufacturing company that sold very large interactive light displays to both businesses and wealthy individuals. The owner asked how he could get more business in the door, thinking he had exhausted all his options. I suggested two simple ideas:

1. Send past customers a free box of parts that commonly wear out with use over time along with a simple thank you for being a customer. No selling language, just a gesture of gratitude.
2. Include the plant manager in his next marketing session to see if they had any ideas for new campaigns. (At first, the owner balked at the idea, telling me his plant manager was an engineer, not a marketing person. All I said in response was, "He touches your product every single day. You don't think he's had an idea or two as to how to sell it?")

The results:

1. Past customers called to thank him for his kind gesture and started to buy more displays as well as referring him to their networks.
2. The plant manager helped both the salespeople and marketing team see the product from a different perspective, which helped them create better language that the customer could relate to. Better marketing + better sales language = more revenue!

The overall sales for that year exceeded the owner's expectations and he was a happy camper!

What's the Difference?

There is a distinct difference between marketing and selling. Let's go back to KNOW | LIKE | TRUST again and review where marketing ends, and sales begin.

KNOW is creating brand awareness for your target audience. LIKE is creating content that resonates with your target audience. TRUST is where they LIKE you so much, they trust you enough to give you money for your product/service.

Selling happens between LIKE and TRUST. Your marketing team will have a much more robust message if the sales team tells marketing what prospects and customers need, finding better leads and more closed sales.

To illustrate the difference between these two functions, here are the overarching duties of each role.

MARKETING	SALES
Creates brand awareness	Develops relationships with prospects
Produces content that attract leads	Wide knowledge of company's offerings, including products sold and customer service
Generates engagement with the right prospects	Ability to confidently differentiate company's strengths from competition
Strengthens internal communications	Offers solutions to fit prospects' needs
Measures results of campaigns	Proposes win/win solutions for both parties

Two separate functions headed in one direction…growth!

#RebelMindset: If you only focus on the money, you lose sight of the customer's experience and in the end, you lose out on the sale or worse, repeat customers. It's not about the money!

Why Do They Call It a Sales Funnel?

Whether you have a product or a service or whether it's B2B or B2C, the buyer goes through a process as they engage with you. In business development terms, this is called the sales funnel ('cuz it looks like a funnel…). As your target audience moves through the funnel, the uninterested ones fall out of the funnel and the funnel narrows,leaving you with an audience that is more qualified to be a potential customer.

KNOW: For both B2B and B2C, AWARENESS happens at the very top of the funnel for your target audience. You want your target audience to be aware that you exist. As your audience flows through the funnel, they either fall out or continue based on whether or not they perceive that you can help them. This leads us to LIKE.

LIKE: What you say piques your audience's INTEREST. This is when they become curious about what you sell through your marketing content and messaging. You have grabbed their attention and they want to know more. B2B will move to CONSIDERATION and INTENT, while B2C will move to DESIRE based on what they are hearing and seeing about your product/service.

TRUST: B2B customers traditionally move much slower than B2C. This is because there are usually higher costs as well as multiple people involved in the decision-making process associated with B2B products or services. However, once B2C customers have an interest and desire, it's a short trip to taking action to buy.

Selling 101

Selling is intimidating if you let it be! Stop thinking of a prospect or sales call as "selling" – instead, think of it as informing.

HubSpot's definition of selling is technically accurate (see side box), yet it misses one very important part of selling: passion. Passion for what you sell is a crucial part of being good at sales.

Let me tell you about my friend Jeanne. I have known her since the sixth grade, and she has been "selling"since the day I met her! She is the one friend whom I would call the "instigator"or the one with all the ideas of what to do next.

> *HubSpot's[1] definition of selling: Selling is any transaction in which money is exchanged for a good or service. During a sales negotiation, the seller attempts to convince or "sell" the buyer on the benefits of their offer. If the buyer wishes to strike a deal, they will give the seller an agreed upon amount of money in exchange for the seller's product/service. Put simply, selling is the act of persuading.*

She has a degree in human resource management, was in that field for many years, and she was good at it! She was awesome at recruiting, creating organizational engagements, process improvement, and so on. She was never taught the ABCs of selling or had any sales trainings. What she did was talk with passion about the things she believed in and provided evidence of how the internal initiatives would improve retention and productivity amongst the team members.

Today, Jeanne owns the cutest shop in West Bend, Wisconsin,called Savoring Thyme. I have watched her time and time again help her customers find something they would love for themselves or as a gift for others. If Jeanne does not have what a customer needs, she will order it for them or sends them to another shop where she knows they can find exactly what they are looking for. Now that is customer service!

---

[1] https://blog.hubspot.com/sales/definition-of-selling

In both situations, whether she was working as an HR exec or selling items at her store, Jeanne sells simply by using active listening to find the need, create solutions to fill the need, and tell her story with passion and conviction.

You can do the same, I promise! Here is one way to practice: Set up a meeting with a friend and simply talk about what you do and why you love to do it. Within that conversation, you will find words, phrases, and success stories that you can then use in a selling situation. Just talk with the same passion and conviction as you did with your friend.

> **#RebelMindset: If your memory is as bad as mine can be, record the conversation or have your friend write down the words and phrases that resonated with them as you talk.**

Go to the back of this chapter and write down five reasons your solution is the best solution for your customers. Be specific! For example: don't write down, "great customer service." What about your customer service makes it so great?

It's Not About the Money

This is where you and I may disagree with each other, and that's okay. My philosophy about making money is simple: Do great work for a fair price and the money will come. That's it. If your customers don't find value in what you sell, then they won't be customers for long and you will have to keep finding more and more customers to sell to… and that sounds exhausting!

If you feel that what you do is all about the money, then I am shocked you have made it this far into the book! Not kidding…SHOCKED!

Passion. Information. Storytelling. Not selling.

> *"Sell the benefit, not your company or the product.*
> *People buy results, not features."*
> — JAY ABRAHAM

Which of these two signs tells the better story?

Think of selling this way...instead of entering a sales or prospect meeting with apprehension, sweaty palms, and butterflies in your stomach...go in with the mindset of "I'm going to listen first, tell my story, let them know what I do and how I help my customers."

#RebelMindset: Selling is simply telling your story to others.

Remember, we are all adults here, so enter every sales conversation as if you will BOTH end up with a mutually beneficial relationship. You will get paid a fair price and they will get a great service/product in return.

The best way to have a great sales call is to be prepared! If you are Googling the person and organization you are meeting with only five minutes before the sales meeting, you have already lost.

The best way to make a great first impression is to be prepared with the following:

- Clear message
- Sales materials
- Research
- Both ears open

Be Prepared

Having a clear message is knowing exactly what to say about what makes you different from your competition, how you can help them solve their problems, and what makes a mutually beneficial partnership with them.

Knowing what to say during your first conversation with a prospect will leave a great impression. Be prepared to share the following:

- Your experience and how what you have done in the past is relatable to their situation.
- Tell a story about a current or past customer that you helped and the positive outcomes as a result of working with you.
- Know what makes you different from your competition. This is your unique selling proposition (USP) that you wrote earlier in this book.

> **#RebelMindset: Your USP is much different than slamming your competition. Think of it as rising above them vs. putting them below you.**

Sales materials include sales sheets/brochures, examples of products, blank contracts, logoed material, etc. I used to have what my boss called "the magic folder." It had sales sheets/brochures, business cards, blank sample contracts, a sample training manual, logoed pens/journal... everything! I kept one in my computer bag and one in my car (because you never know when an opportunity will present itself). No matter where the conversation went on the needs of the customer, I had the material to support it.

Your first meeting (I like to call it a "Discovery Meeting") with a prospect is not the time to ask questions that you could already know by searching the World Wide Web. Using the phrase, "according to some research I did on your company/you, I understand that..." is very powerful. It shows the person you are talking to you didn't just show up, you took the time to do your homework. A follow-up question to this is, "Is this a true representation of your organization/ you?" Because we all know that if it's on the internet, it's true! NOT!

You Don't Know What You Don't Know

Have an open mind. You may enter the sales meeting already predicting how it will go and what they will buy. That is great for a starter to the conversation, yet I have been in LOTS of sales conversations that lead down a very different path than I anticipated.

You have two ears and one mouth, use them proportionally. Oftentimes it turns out that the customer doesn't even know what they truly need. You will be talking about a product/service you offer, and they say a key word or phrase that triggers a completely different need they have that you can solve.

For example, I had a customer who hired me to create a comprehensive marketing strategy for their customers that were in a multitude of industries, with each industry having their own jargon and ways of buying their products. As I met with the head of each department, it was clear that more marketing was not going to fix their declining sales issue. Based on what I had been hearing, I did a customer experience analysis and discovered that they were losing sales due to poor e-commerce application and an outdated website. Both were difficult to navigate. It was hard to find specific products on their website and some of their most popular products were not even listed on the site. On top of that, once the product was found, their e-commerce application was slow and had way too many hoops to jump through before their customer could hit the "buy" button.

What started as a marketing strategy customer turned into a complete overhaul of their customer experience. This included the internal customer experience. They had gotten so busy fixing all their customer's complaints, they forgot to talk to each other! Operations didn't know what the sales team was presenting, and once a sale was made, it wasn't until the orders showed up that production knew the customer existed!

In the end, their new website is beautiful and easy to navigate, their e-commerce has fewer hoops to get to the buy button, their internal teams are communicating with one another more often and leadership has incorporated weekly one-to-one meetings with each department head to stay abreast of challenges and, more importantly, the wins that they can celebrate!

Lesson Learned

We all know that person who dominates a conversation and always turns the topic back to themselves. (You are picturing a person in your network right now, aren't you?) I fully admit I used to be one of those people! Being the youngest of six kids, I rarely got a word in edgewise. When I left for college, it was nice not to have to talk over my big brothers and sisters, so I talked…a lot…and fast. My good friend Carole used to say, "*Lisa, I can't listen as fast as you talk.*"

Over the years of being both in sales/marketing and consulting, I have learned to slow my pace and to (simply put) shut up and listen. This tactic is also very helpful for raising teenagers. If you listen more than speak, they will share a lot more than if you are continuously telling them, "This is what I did as a kid in your situation" or "If I were you, this is what I would do." They will never be able to solve their own problems if you keep talking. Sorry, this is a business book, yet the same listening method works in both parenting and in business. Ask the question, then stop talking.

Research done in 1972[2] regarding "wait time" in education talks about the time it takes for students to process a question and be able to answer it. On average, teachers wait only 1.5 seconds after asking a question before moving on. The concept of "wait time" in teaching is still used today.

"Wait time" in business is critical. Recently, I was listening to a podcast and the speaker noted it takes an average of 8-10 seconds for an adult to process a question and form a response. How long do you wait before you start talking after asking a question? During a pause you probably start thinking: "They aren't answering, so I may need to rephrase the question." No, just let them think! Silence is golden here. Be patient. Next time you are in a conversation and ask a question, be cognizant of how long you wait for a response.

Here are some benefits you may find from waiting eight seconds:

- With employees – You'll get better information than you will if you press them to provide a quick answer. You hired them for their expertise. Do what you can to let them share it. In return they'll know they are valued.
- When selling – You will often get to hear about deeper problems even they don't know they have if you give them some time. This will provide you with a window into additional value you can provide. Listening closely will help you understand if there is a gap between what they are asking for and what they actually need.

---

[2] https://eric.ed.gov/?id=ED061103

Digital Dementia

In a world of immediate gratification and what scientists call "digital dementia,"[3] we are losing our ability to wait or stick with something through to the end, (so thank you for reading up until this point).

Going forward, take note of your listening skills both at the office and at home. How are you doing? Are you waiting for the other person to form their answer or are you jumping in with another question?

Here are a few tips to improve your listening skills and the information you learn when you ask a question:

1. First and foremost, put away your phone and laptop so they are out of sight.
2. Face the person you are talking to. (Yes, this is something some people **don't** do.)
3. Relax, smile, and make eye contact.
4. If you need to take notes, ask if it's okay first to show respect.
5. Practice active listening. Do not think of your next meeting or wonder where you should have lunch or if you need to pick up milk on the way home. Just listen.
6. Listen to learn, not to respond, and ask clarifying questions so you fully understand what they are trying to tell you.
7. Are you doing all the talking? Have a trigger to stop yourself, even if it's putting your hand over your mouth. (Be discrete, you don't need to look like one of the Three Wise Monkeys)
8. Enjoy the conversation. Effective communication is an art form and is only fine-tuned by practicing.
9. And lastly, cut yourself some slack. So, what if you didn't say EXACTLY what you wanted to say the moment you wanted to say it. It's okay.

---

[3] https://www.youtube.com/watch?v=fJPkxDje5p8&t=35s

Now, I will admit there are times I still dominate conversations. When I catch myself, I stop, apologize, ask the other person a question and literally cover my mouth with my hand as a reminder to shut up and listen.

Two ears, one mouth…have fun using them proportionately!! It is amazing what you can learn from someone else when you take the time to listen.

Review Your RebelMindset

- Selling is simply informing and storytelling.
- Practice active listening to hear the real needs of the customer.
- Be authentic and sell with passion and conviction.

Chapter 7 Worksheet:

Who in your organization oversees:

Marketing: _____

Selling: _____

What ways can they work collaboratively for the betterment of the organization?

What makes your product/service better than the competition?

1.

2.

3.

4.

5.

CHAPTER 8

The Power of Giving

"Only by giving are you able to receive
more than you already have."
—JIM ROHN

This chapter was originally going to be about referrals and how to monetize them by building referral programs within your network. As I was typing, it felt wrong; I was writing words that go against every fiber in my being! So, I quickly deleted what I wrote and started writing about what I have always believed in: "It is better to give than to receive."

Now, I know there are plenty of you who will disagree with me about this, which makes it all the more fun to write this chapter! (I'm typing this with a relatively devilish look on my face.)

You are saying, "Lisa, you are leaving money on the table!"

It's not about the money.

Oooooh, I can envision some of you flinching! If that is the case, then you may want to go back and reread Chapter 7! Being in business is NOT only about the money.

The intent of this chapter is finding out how to grow your network and grow your business through giving. There is no worksheet for this chapter, yet you may want to grab your highlighter for the B.A.N.T. section.

Introductions, Referrals, and Recommendations

First, let's define what each one of these is before we discuss the give vs receive component of growing your business.

Introductions: When you introduce two people who may have something in common and the connection is mutually beneficial, they can decide if it is a good connection or not.

Referral: When someone is seeking a product or service, you refer them to resources you know can fulfill their need and let that person make their own choice whether to use that resource.

Recommendation: This is when you recommend someone to a person or organization you trust, where you can be sure that they are sincere and are in the position to offer the exact service required to solve a need. Your reputation is on the line with this one.

In each of these circumstances, you need to do your homework and understand that whether it's a negative or positive outcome, it will reflect on you. Choose wisely.

As a recipient of the introduction/referral/recommendation, it is vitally important to acknowledge and thank the person doing the introductions. More importantly, it is crucial to reach out as soon as possible to the person you are being introduced to. If you wait, it reflects poorly on you...and worse, it reflects poorly on the person doing the introducing.

Not responding quickly is the fastest way to be crossed off the recommendations list!

Referrals & Recommendations Lead to Faster Sales

There is no faster way to grow your business than through referrals and recommendations. This approach skips the process of making your target audience pay attention to your marketing and remember your brand. It saves the buyer time in researching how to solve their problem and helps the buyer get to "yes" faster in the sales process.

According to a HubSpot article[1], there are nine reasons referrals are your best sales opportunity.

1) Lower Cost
Referrals cost you nothing to acquire, and it would be appropriate to send a small thank-you gift to the person doing the referring.

2) More Trust
You start the relationship at a higher point of trust. When you meet a new prospect for the first time, you need to show up "trustworthy." Referrals are considered "borrowed trust."

3) Fewer Pricing Objections
While conversations about your price or fee are never off the table, when you work from referrals, people are almost always willing to pay a little more when you've been recommended by someone they trust.

4) Faster Process
Most sales that start with a referral move through the sales funnel faster because they start from a higher trust factor. Many prospects come intending to do business with you.

5) Easier Closes
Your "closing ratio" is notably higher. A number of businesses experience 10 to 30 percent higher closing ratios than from other lead sources. Referral-based sales usually close at 50 to 70 percent.

6) Bigger Sales
Your sales are often larger, as the buyer has a higher trust level with you.

---

[1] https://blog.hubspot.com/sales/reasons-referrals-are-your-best-sales-opportunities

7) Advisor Status
Prospects and customers you meet through referrals are most likely to
follow your suggestions based on the fact they know their friend or
colleague has had a good experience.

8) More Referrals
Positive results produce more referrals. A customer obtained through
a referral is more likely to refer you to someone else.

9) Fun
It's a fun way to create more leads!

**#RebelMindset: The more referrals you give, the more
likely you are to receive them!**

The Benefits of Giving

Do you have "takers" in your network? You know, those people who
always seem to be asking for something and say they'll return the favor,
yet never do. They are usually the people you see at a networking
event and when you see them your first thought is to figure out how
to avoid them. And I bet you are picturing one of those people in
your mind right now. (I am.)

Studies[2] show that giving causes positive biological reactions in
humans; we secrete feel-good chemicals, such as serotonin, dopamine,
and oxytocin in our brains. Scientists have also found that giving stim-
ulates the mesolimbic pathway, which is the reward center in the brain,
releasing endorphins and creating what is known as the "helper's high."

Studies also show that giving has physical and mental benefits like:

- Lowering blood pressure
- Increasing self-esteem

---

[2] https://health.clevelandclinic.org/why-giving-is-good-for-your-health/

- Lessening depression
- Lowering stress levels
- Elongating life
- Increasing happiness and satisfaction

Giving is not only good for business, it is good for your mind and body! WIN/WIN!

> **#RebelMindset: Think about your networking activities in the past three months. Are you a giver or a taker? Going forward, be only a giver and see how good it feels!**

Hot or Not?

Did you ever play hot and cold when you were a kid? Someone would hide an object and you would find the object by receiving verbal cues of "warm" if you were headed in the right direction, "cold" if you were not, or "hot" if you were right next to it. The same goes for giving or receiving leads.

Knowing the temperature of your lead helps you determine how much time and effort you need to spend pursuing it.

Reminder: "LEAD" is defined as a company or person who has expressed interest and has the potential of becoming a customer, aka: a prospect.

Cold Lead: also known as an unqualified lead. Cold leads have usually never heard of you, need to be educated about what you sell, and persuaded that they need to buy from you. These leads can be found at the top of your sales funnel.

Warm Lead: These leads have shown some interest in what you have to offer. They know you exist yet may be buying from your competition. These leads usually don't need to be convinced to buy what you sell; they just need to be convinced to buy from you instead of your competition. These leads can be found in the middle of the sales funnel.

Hot Leads: also known as qualified leads. Hot leads know they need your product or service, are interested in your organization, and able to buy from you very soon. These leads are practically falling out the bottom of the sales funnel.

Which one sounds like the most fun to give and receive?

Qualifying Your Leads

Once you have a lead in your hand, what are you to do with it? The first thing to do is qualify the lead. You can do that by utilizing B.A.N.T., originally created by IBM®.

This is an acronym for:

- **B**udget: do they have enough money to spend on your product/ service?
- **A**uthority: are you talking to the person who can make the decision to buy?
- **N**eed: how long has the prospect needed your product/service?
- **T**iming: how quickly do they want what you sell implemented?

Here are some questions you can either ask the person who gave you the lead or during the initial conversation with your new prospect.

BUDGET

- What do you currently spend on _____? (insert your product or service here)
  - o If spending money on what you sell is new to them, go to the NEED questions.

- What is the cost of trying to solve this problem internally vs outsourcing it?
  - o This is a good question for subject matter experts who can quickly solve the problem vs the prospect trying to do it internally.

- What is the cost of doing nothing? What will the problem look like in three years?
  - ○ There may be a ripple effect in doing nothing. What other people or departments will be negatively affected if the problem does not get solved? It may cost more money to fix the problem at a later date.

AUTHORITY

- Who will be using the product/service?
  - ○ This will give you who the end users are within an organization; these people could also be influencers in on the buying decision.
- Who else needs to be included in our conversation to help with the decision-making process?
  - ○ It is better to tell the story yourself than rely on your prospect to represent you to other internal stakeholders.
- When was the last time you purchased this product/service?
  - ○ This will lead you to the timing questions as well as knowing if that person made the decision last time.

NEED

- When did you realize you had this problem to solve?
  - ○ Knowing if this is a new problem or one that has been around a long time will help you determine the severity of the problem.
- What steps have you already taken to fix the problem?
  - ○ Did they try to solve it internally or use an outside source that failed to fix the problem? Knowing this will help you to understand if they will have concerns on the reliability of your organization to fix the problem.

- How high is this purchase on your priority list?
  - o Are they willing to move quickly or are they just window-shopping?

TIMING

- Do you have a deadline you are trying to meet?
  - o This lets you know the urgency and if you can fulfill it.

- Q4: Sometimes organizations need to use what's left of their budget or they won't get the same amount to spend next year.
  - o If you have a product they can stock or prepurchase a service for the upcoming year, Q4 is a great time to find and give leads.

- What time of year do you make this purchase?
  - o This is a good question for organizations that have busy seasons. They may have more money to spend during the busy months, or they have more time to implement during the slower months.

Highlight the questions that pertain to qualifying your prospects. Better yet…write your own questions for B.A.N.T. that apply to your specific industry. The more the questions sound like you vs like a robot reading from a script, it will make asking them easier and the information you get will be more qualified!

> **#RebelMindset: These are merely suggestions to help the sales conversation along. Please do not pepper someone with a multitude of questions like they are under a spotlight in an interrogation room. They are a prospect, not a criminal.**

Go Fish! No worms required.

Social media channels have practically eliminated the six degrees of separation theory originally set out by Frigyes Karinthy in 1929 and popularized by a 1990 play written by John Guare. Yet, being so easily accessible to anyone has caused an additional barrier to be built, safeguarding ourselves against spam and the "pitch" messages.

That is when it is time to play a little Go Fish!

Grab your friends, co-workers, networking partners, trusted vendors, centers of influence,or anyone else whom you feel would give you a quality introduction to your targeted list of prospects and play Go Fish with LinkedIn.

There are a few things you need to prepare before you start playing.

- Be honest with the people you are meeting and tell them you are having the conversation to ask for introductions to their contact(s).

- Know your ideal customer profile; we did this in Chapter 4, so you are all set. Have your list of specific organizations or individuals you want to meet.

- Find a way to reciprocate by buying them lunch or introducing them to contacts that fit their ideal customer profile. (If they don't know who their ideal customer is, buy them a copy of this book! Admittedly… a shameless plug!)

- Be respectful of their relationship between your connection and the person they are introducing you to by following some simple rules:

  o Don't be a pushy salesperson. Ever.

  o Respect the timing of the other person's calendar; be patient.

  o Be on time and come prepared with great questions about their organization and the B.A.N.T. questions.

  o Follow up with a kind thank-you note or gift, If possible, handwritten and mailed; it leaves a great impression vs an email.

  o If you need to follow up at a different time, mark it in your calendar and do it in the manner they asked you to.

Gatekeepers and "we already have a (your product/service here)" can stop us cold when trying to pitch our product/service to our ideal prospects. It's a game of "who you know" in today's networking world to break through the barriers in some organizations.

> **#RebelMindset: Willingly accept the word NO...it is 100 percent up to your friend if they will connect you. It may be that the relationship has not solidified on their end yet, so be patient and considerate of their reasoning.**

MOST IMPORTANT: Follow up immediately once your friend sends the introduction! Be professional and respectful to not taint the relationship your friend has already established with this contact. The relationship with this new contact is on the line as well as the one with your friend.

Celebrate! Whether it is simply an introductory meeting or closed business with this new connection, take your friend out for lunch or a drink to say thank you!

I have seen this work. Be sure to invite only those you trust, and you know will make a great impression on your connections. Your reputation is at stake here, choose wisely and have some fun with it!

Good luck and GO FISH!!

Golden Rule of Networking

"My Golden Rule of Networking is simple: Don't keep score."
— HARVEY MACKAY

Networking is about building relationships, not building your Rolodex®...wait, I am dating myself...not building your CRM's contact list. The person with the most contacts does not win. The person with the most targeted and qualified list wins. Don't be greedy!

Review Your RebelMindset:

- Use B.A.N.T. to qualify leads.
- Go Fish! is not just for kids anymore.
- Keeping score is forbidden in this game.

CHAPTER 9

Marketing Is a Team Sport

Picture this: Members of your team are having lunch at a local restaurant. They are chatting about work when someone at the next table overhears them using keywords from your industry. That person starts a conversation with your team, asking questions to learn more about your organization and your team says, "Not sure, that is sales' job" – and POOF! that opportunity is lost.

Now picture your team in the same lunchtime situation, yet instead, they respond with something like this: "Yes, we do offer those solutions and we have several customers in your vertical that we have helped in the past. Would it be okay if I took your business card and had someone from our business development team give you a call to discuss this further?"

Which one do you think will lead to a sale?

> *Before you start panicking that this is happening at your organization, go to rebelgirlmarketing.com/guide and download your Chapter 9 worksheet. We will be talking strategies to keep your team informed.*

> *"Growth is never by mere chance; it is the result of forces working together."*
> —JAMES CASH PENNEY

Build a Culture of Brand Ambassadors

When your team is fully informed as to who is within your ideal customer profile, what problems you solve, and feel they are well informed on what is happening in your organization, two very important things will happen:

1. Your entire team will be more engaged with your organization
    a. Leading to loyalty (less turnover)
    b. Brand championing (brand awareness)
2. Increased number of qualified leads
    a. More sales meetings
    b. Increased revenue

I have seen how effective this strategy is firsthand at organizations I have worked at in the past (and I teach this strategy to my customers). Leadership offers quarterly company wide teleconference meetings to hear about how the organization is doing financially, informing them of new product launches, sharing success stories, giving them a heads-up on marketing campaigns…(you get the idea). These quarterly gatherings built an entire organization of brand champions. Now, instead of relying on your sales team and marketing campaigns to get the word out, each of your team members become committed to furthering the success of your brand.

Now, I am not saying you need to share your P&L statements or your tax returns with them, be logical. Yet, when you launch a new product or marketing campaign, does your team hear it from you first…or Facebook?

Go to your worksheet or the back of this chapter and rank yourself on how well you do keeping your team informed about the following topics:

- What you sell – both tangible and intangible
- Whom you sell it to – your ideal customer profile
- What to say if asked what your company does

- New products being launched
- Upcoming marketing and/or sales campaigns
- How the company is doing
- Changes in their benefits

> **#RebelMindset: Leadership is not about authority. Leadership is about creating opportunities for your team's growth and creating more leaders. You can do that by being transparent.**

Internal Marketing

If you ask a business owner what their biggest challenge is in today's work environment, it will more than likely have to do with talent... the retaining, training, engaging, hiring, and productivity of people. The way we work today is much different for most organizations than it was at the beginning of 2020. It's time to rethink how, where, and when we work.

"Even without remote work, the way we work in person will likely never be quite the same. Finding, hiring, and engaging with employees is different in a world where remote is becoming more and more common. Are you prepared to reimagine your office spaces and the way you engage with your employees?" (from a January 2021 article by Daisy Ein)[1]

I have noticed that some organizations spend the majority of their time focusing on making external customers happy, they forget about their internal customers, their team. This is a lot like the which came first query, the chicken or the egg?

> **#RebelMindset: Internal marketing is simply about making sure your team is informed.**

---

[1] https://business.tutsplus.com/articles/business-challenges-and-hr-trends--cms-36386

Not buying it? One of the most successful men in our time, Richard Branson, is quoted as saying, *"Clients do not come first. Employees come first. If you take care of your employees, they will take care of the clients."*

Internal marketing is a communication strategy to keep every team member within your organization feeling informed and included. Here are some examples of what to incorporate into your internal marketing strategy:

- Review the organization's overall goals and strategies.
    - **Benefit**: reinforces how their work ties into the greater good of the organization.
- Educate on the organization as a whole, including your products/services and ideal customer profile(s).
    - **Benefit:** creates brand ambassadors.
- Ensure leadership has the employees' as well as the customers' best interests at heart.
    - **Benefit**: ties directly into building a culture of trust.

Still unsure internal marketing is a good idea?

Gallup[2] data shows that only 13 percent of employees strongly agree that the leadership of their organization communicates effectively with the rest of the organization.

13 percent... not good!

There are right and wrong ways to build out your internal marketing strategies. Ask yourself a few vital questions: (compliments of my friends at humanworks)[3]

1. What has been the impact of COVID on internal communications?
2. What are your internal marketing channels? Which need more attention?

---

[2] https://www.gallup.com/workplace/313367/internal-communications-execute-winning-strategy.aspx
[3] //humanworks8.com/

3. What critical elements need to be communicated?

4. How do you know if your communications are working?

Use your worksheet or the back of this chapter to answer these questions and brainstorm how to improve on each area. What else matters to your team?

> **#RebelMindset: Make sure your internal customers matter just as much (if not more) than your external customers.**

Don't Forget the Fun

If you Google "sense of humor in business," you will get over 119 million search results. Why? Because people are talking about it… a lot… and not because it is so prevalent in the workplace. Sources like ***INC***[4], ***Forbes***[5], ***Harvard Business Review***[6], ***Stanford Graduate School of Business***[7] and ***Business Insider***[8] are all saying the same thing about the benefits of having a sense of humor at work:

- There is a serious lack of humor at work
- It is highly effective for employee engagement and retention
- Productivity increases
- Increases innovation and inspiration
- It improves mood, reduces blood pressure, and decreases stress
- The most successful organizations use humor inside the office and in their marketing

---

[4] https://www.inc.com/tim-askew/success-and-humor.html

[5] https://www.forbes.com/sites/steveolenski/2018/06/15/the-cmos-guide-to-using-humor-in-marketing/?sh=311ff8d562bf

[6] https://hbr.org/2017/09/how-to-rediscover-your-inspiration-at-work?autocomplete=true

[7] https://www.gsb.stanford.edu/insights/humor-serious-business

[8] https://www.businessinsider.com/a-sense-of-humor-could-mean-youre-healthier-happier-and-smarter-2017-10

Humor can be defined in many ways, yet there are guidelines as to what NOT to do in a work environment such as not making fun of someone else – their work, their physical appearance, etc.

#RebelMindset: If it is only funny to you, don't say it.

Not sure where to start? Start small. Pick an internal meeting and toss in a few humorous quotes or industry-related cartoons to kick off the meeting or presentation. If your organization has recently done a video for social or your website, ask your videographer to pull together a blooper reel and show it during an all-staff meeting. Or, just smile more. A simple smile can go along way!

Feel free to steal this idea: Where I used to work, we made up silly titles for our workspace nameplates. As the marketing director, my nameplate read "Propaganda Princess" and our controller was "Kicker of Assets" – it made you smile just walking into our offices.

Start each day on a positive note. Maybe on the way to work, turn off the news radio and turn on a comedy station on your satellite radio. Wouldn't it be nice to start your day smiling and laughing instead of stressed out and irritated? (Or, is it only me that gets irritated when I listen to news radio??)

Still not convinced that humor works? Tell me if you know which B2C companies these sayings★ are from that have NOTHING to do with their products:

- Dilly, Dilly!
- Mike, Mike, Mike, Mike, Mike, Mike, Mike, Mike, Mike!!
- Fahrvergnugen (that one is for my Baby Boomer and Gen X friends)

Have I made my point yet?

On your worksheet, list a few places where you can insert humor into your workday. If being humorous is not in your wheelhouse, then recruit someone from your team and ask them to bring you ideas as to how to incorporate more fun into your organization.

To get you started, here are a few ideas:

- Post a joke of the day on a whiteboard. (Keep it clean, HR is in the house…)
- Host a happy hour at a local pub.
- Working remotely? Host a virtual happy hour with a trivia game.
- Form a company team to do a charity walk.
- Host a family day at your local baseball team's game.
- Bring lunch for your team and insist they eat it anywhere but at their desk.
- Holiday attire day: pick any national holiday, encourage people to dress up and hold a costume contest.

See the End Notes to find the articles mentioned above. And as a bonus, spend 11 minutes watching this video: Humor at work | Andrew Tarvin | TEDx Ohio State[9] University. I promise you will not regret it!

★Bud Light®, Geico® Insurance, Volkswagen®

Employer Branding Matters

Employer branding is how you manage and influence your reputation as an employer among job seekers and employees. When your employer brand is associated with a positive company culture, there are a number of benefits, starting with these:

- Employer brand is the difference between top candidates searching for a new career opportunity via online search vs. going directly to the career page on your website because they want to specifically work for you.

---

[9] https://www.youtube.com/watch?v=6iFCm5ZokBI

- You don't want candidates to see your employment posting as "just another job." You want them to see you as a long-term career solution and to resonate with your culture.
- Customers are more likely to buy your product if they know you treat your team well.
- Retention starts as early as the recruiting process. You want candidates and new hires to feel connected to your culture and become brand ambassadors.

When you build a great company culture, your team and customers talk about it. Grab your worksheet and answer these questions:

1. Why would someone want to work for you?
2. What is the perception your employees have about you as an employer?
3. Do job seekers know who you are?
4. Would your team recommend your company as a great place to work?

If you do not have the answers to these questions, then it is important to grab your leadership team and figure out how you want to be perceived as an employer. What steps can you take to make sure you become an employer of choice?

RebelMindset: Marketing is a team sport!

There are so many ways you can become an employer of choice; it simply takes intentionality. Be patient and remember that your brand is developed over time, and it will take your team some time to get used to changing how you do business internally. Start slow, don't give up, and ask for input from your team as to ways to improve your company's culture.

The risk is worth the reward!

Review Your RebelMindset

- Build brand ambassadors.
- Make sure your team knows your story.
- Become an employer of choice.

Chapter 9 Worksheet:

How well do I communicate with my team?

1 = oh crap!   4 = I'm a rockstar!

I inform my entire team about:	Ranking			
What we sell – both tangible and intangible	1	2	3	4
Who we sell it to – your ideal customer profile	1	2	3	4
What to say if asked what your company does	1	2	3	4
New products being launched	1	2	3	4
Upcoming marketing and/or sales campaigns	1	2	3	4
How the company is doing - financially	1	2	3	4
How the company is doing – meeting sales goals	1	2	3	4
Changes in their benefits	1	2	3	4
Brainstorming for new ideas	1	2	3	4
	1	2	3	4
	1	2	3	4
	1	2	3	4

What needs to be included in your internal marketing communications?

1. What has been the impact of COVID on internal communications?

2. What are your internal marketing channels? Which need more attention?

3. What critical elements need to be communicated?

4. How do you know if your communications are working?

5. What else?

Bring on the Fun!

Who will lead this initiative? _____

List a few ideas here:

-

-

-

-

-

Employer Branding Questions:

1. Why would someone want to work for you?

2. What is the perception your employees have about you as an employer?

3. Do job seekers know who you are?

4. Would your team recommend your company as a great place to work?

CHAPTER 10

Networking on Purpose

> **#RebelMindset: Networking is a key component of your overall marketing strategy; it just needs to be done with intentionality.**

Time Is Money and Money Is Money

Let's face it, networking can be a time suck. We schedule an in-person networking meeting that you think is only going to be one hour out of your day, right? Nope, it's a lot more than one hour.

Think of the time you spend prepping for the meeting, driving to and from the meeting location, and the follow-up emails and calls. All that time spent networking is lost productive time. Not only it is lost time but attending networking events costs actual money. You spend money on the cost of an event, the cost of the membership, coffees, lunches, adult beverages, etc. It can add up quickly.

At this point, it would be easy to say to just skip networking altogether and do the client work that makes you money. Yet, it's not about the money! (You may be sensing a theme by now.)

Networking Works!

Near the beginning of Rebel Girl Marketing, I took a time-management class (recommended by a friend, just like in Chapter 8…

151

recommendations work). The class was fun, the trainer was an amazing public speaker, and her time-management strategies were fantastic!

After her class, the trainer and time-management guru, Taren, and I started chatting. She told me about an incident she recently encountered at a networking event: Taren was having a lovely conversation with four other people at a table when a woman came by, flung her business cards at everyone at her table, insisted she collect their business cards, and just walked away; no small talk, no real introduction, she went from table to table collecting business cards this way. The next thing she knew, Taren is on this woman's email list. You can probably imagine how quickly Taren unsubscribed from that list!

I ran into Taren at various networking meetings from time to time, each time we laughed whilst sharing other networking horror stories and discussing the do's and don'ts of networking.

At that time, she was building a series of in-person events, targeting small business owners. Based on our previous conversations, she asked me to be a guest speaker to talk about how to create great elevator pitches. *The Power of Your Pitch* was born and is still my most popular speaking topic to date.

Thanks to Taren, my speaking career was launched!

The point of this story is networking works. If it wasn't for our conversations about networking…during networking…my public speaking career may never have launched. From there, she and I have created several other topics (including the topic of *Networking on Purpose*).

Networking, done well, can lead your career to places you never thought you could go…you just need to show up!

For more information on Taren, you can find out more at:

Taren Sartler

Consultant, Speaker, Goddess of Time
Tick Tock It's About Time LLC

www.ticktockitstime.com
262-701-7870

Last time! Head to rebelgirlmarketing.com/guide to get your PDF for the Chapter 10 worksheet or head to the end of this chapter for the worksheet section. You will be creating a list of where to network using the Power Pitches you created in Chapter 5.

Network on Purpose

Why do we network? Most people think the only reason to network is to gain leads. I'd like to shift your mindset about networking. In my opinion, there are three reasons to network:

1. Lead Generation
2. Community
3. Education

Lead Generation: This is where you go to find leads to grow your business and more importantly, give leads. There are some groups that are strictly lead-generation organizations. These are good for B2C sales where there is a high volume of transactions. For B2B organizations, this is where your strategic partners hang out. Again, it does not need to be a formal organization. You can create a group yourself and invite those you want to network with. It's all about aligning yourself with relationships that are mutually beneficial and filling your sales funnel... over time.

Community: In this work-at-home, remote life we have these days, it's good to have a sense of community. That community is more than the people who work at your office or within your organization; this is where you find like-minded people who can support you. It is somewhere you can go to talk out challenges you are having and celebrate your wins! Your community is filled with people who are there to keep you going when you feel like quitting. This does not need to be a formal organization. It could simply be a group of people who meet regularly to support one another.

Education: Networking for education is extremely important. It's not just about keeping up with the changes in your industry either. Learning how to be better at specific skills like computer programs you use on a regular basis, how to be a better leader, how to work with other industry groups, understanding diversity and inclusion, learning about industries you sell to or buy from, and the list goes on. Becoming better at what you do is not just about your day-to-day "job" – it's about being easier to work with, a better communicator or even reading this book, how to better market and sell our products/services. It is never too late to learn, and it is never too early to get a jump on being a better overall human being.

> **#RebelMindset: Never stop learning, never stop growing as a professional, and keep an open mind as to other ways of doing business.**

To help you organize where to network on purpose, there is a table like the one below on your worksheet and at the end of this chapter that will help you decide the best places to spend your time and money to gain leads, find your community, and keep learning.

Lead Generation	Community	Education
Places	Places	Places
People	People	People
Pitch	Pitch	Pitch

Under each of the three categories, you will be filling in the following:

Places: What organizations, associations, or networking groups fit into each of those categories? You can even take it a step further and write down when they meet and the annual cost of being a member/attendee.

People: Whom do you know that is already a member or has been a past member of the group? If you don't know anyone, look up the email or phone number of whom you can talk to at that organization to gain more information and attend a meeting as a guest – "try before you buy" kind of thing. Give that person a call, set up a meeting to find out how that organization works and if this is the place you'd like to consider joining.

Pitch: You wouldn't use the same pitch for lead-gen that you would use for education networking, so be sure to write a pitch for each category. Go back to your worksheet from Chapter 5 to find your Power words and create something that will resonate with that audience.

Here is the example I have for my own business, just not listing people as there are too many to list at this point!

Lead Generation	Community	Education
Places: Idea Collective: weekly options #GirlBosses: 3x/month Encompass: 1x/month Cigar Networkers: 1x/month	Places: Idea Collective: weekly options #GirlBossses: 3x/month Encompass: 1x/month Power of Your Journey: annually	Places: American Marketing Association (as a marketing professional) Idea Collective (as a business owner)
People:	People:	People:
Pitch: *As a marketing strategist, it is my job to make sure that when your clients and prospects need what you sell, they think of you first.*	Pitch: *Marketing has become more complicated. My job is to sort through all the noise and create simple, intentional marketing strategies that build brand awareness that result in more sales conversations.*	Pitch: *I help small businesses stay in business by creating strategies that utilize multiple marketing channels, to increase brand awareness that lead to more sales conversations.*

As you can see, there is one place I get all three categories of networking. The Idea Collective Small Business Incubator (ideacollectiveincubator.com) is a place for me to learn as a business owner, gain leads, and most importantly find my sense of community. As a solo entrepreneur, I go there for a boost of inspiration, give back to other members by sharing my industry knowledge, and learn how to be a better business owner.

My time and money are spent strategically each month. I do not attend every single meeting for each of these organizations. I stay active in each of these organizations, yet do not let networking be my only channel of marketing.

> **#RebelMindset: Back in Chapter 8 we talked about The Power of Giving. Networking is where you will apply the principle of giving more than you get and not keeping score.**

"You can have everything in life you want if you will just help enough other people get what they want."
—ZIG ZIGLAR

Networking & KNOW | LIKE | TRUST

Networking is the long-game strategy and the key to great networking is consistency.

Your networking strategy has short-, mid-, and long-term goals that can be directly correlated to the KNOW | LIKE | TRUST that we discussed back in Chapter 1.

KNOW: Short-term goals for networking are for your new connections to get to know you. (KNOW = awareness) You're not going to show up to a networking meeting a couple of times and be asked to be a keynote speaker at their next summit or be given big-time leads right away. People need to get to know who you are, what you stand for, what you sell, and if you are reliable. In the short term, it's about helping others without asking for anything in return. It's about giving free advice to show you are a subject matter expert.

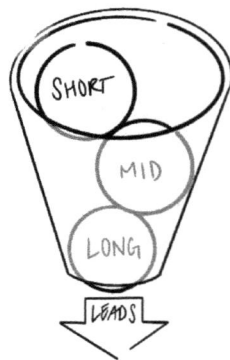

It's about connecting with the people in your network. Schedule one-to-one meetings, ask good questions, find out who they are, and who is there to help others…or who is there only there to gain leads and sell you something (those are not your ideal networking partners).

LIKE: Mid-term goals for networking are to foster relationships and build trust, and they can get to like what you have to say (LIKE = content). The more you show up to the networking events, the more people are going to recognize you and the more people are going to start to trust you. Sometimes they'll ask you to speak as a subject matter expert during meetings or write blogs or maybe do a short speaking gig. This is also where they may ask you to join a sub-group of the organization, like a mastermind or industry group.

You give them a clear understanding of the products or services that you sell and then talk about how you want to be known as a subject matter expert.

TRUST: The long-term goal of a networking event is that you build trust. You'll gain new business and be asked to be a subject matter expert. Organizations that I'm part of have asked me to speak on various aspects of marketing as a subject matter expert. Most of my leads for new customers come from other members and I have given plenty of leads to others as well.

> **#RebelMindset: The more you contribute and give back (versus being a taker), the more trust is going to be built and the more you will gain from being a member.**

It's Networking, Not a Sales Call

If there is one thing that will turn people off when you talk to them, it is selling during a networking event. When entering a networking event, it is best to lead with the following mindset:

- You are there to inform, not sell.
  - o Stop thinking that the person directly in front of you will be buying your product/service. Instead, inform that person as to how you solve problems for your customers, and they will be mentally running through the Rolodex® in their head thinking of someone to introduce you to. This is also a great opportunity to describe what makes an ideal client for your organization.
- Lead with the intention that you will be giving more than you are getting.
  - o At some point in the conversation with each person you talk to, ask, "How can I help?" It will show them that you are there to be a giver, not a taker.
- Strive for one remarkable connection vs many lackluster conversations.
  - o One great connection with someone at a networking event that leads to a discovery meeting and eventually new business is better than superficial conversations with a dozen people.
- HAVE FUN
  - o Just because you are networking, doesn't mean you have to be boring. I am not saying you need to put on a comedy show, yet it is good to show passion for your business and how you help your customers.
- Give yourself permission to leave.
  - o Not all networking events are built the same. If you have to force yourself to be there or you just had a really sh!tty day, give yourself permission to leave. It is better to have no conversation than one that sucks and leaves a bad first impression.

Tips and Tricks to Make a Great First Impression

Networking is not for everyone, I get it. There are times when I have literally sat in my car, ready to drive to a networking event, and had to convince myself to actually go to the event. It would have been easier to go home, put on sweats, grab a glass of wine, and watch *Ted Lasso*; instead, I start my car and go to the event.

Here are some ways I make networking fun and productive:

- Sing myself happy
  - My singing voice is only for when I am driving alone in my car! Even I don't like hearing it, so I crank my favorite tunes and sing out loud all the way to the event. By the time I get there, I am energized and in a good mood, ready to network.
- Ice Breakers: Hygge and/or Barguments (when choosing: know your audience!)
  - Hygge Game has all open-ended questions that make great icebreaker questions. Grab a card or two and put them in your pocket. It's a good way to start a conversation with someone you don't know. Questions rating: G
  - Barguments is a book of questions that have no right or wrong answers. The questions can drum up some interesting conversations and some are just funny and nonsensical. Question rating: PG to R
- When you schedule time for the networking event, schedule 30-45 minutes within the next couple of days to follow up by connecting on LinkedIn, sending an email, etc.
  - This takes the pressure off figuring out what to do next. If it only takes you 15 minutes to do your follow-up, you get to be ahead of schedule that day. Yay!

To Refer or Not to Refer, That Is the Question

As you network, there will be opportunities to give and receive introductions to other people's contacts as a lead for new business. Here is where I ask you to tread lightly. Each person you introduce to others will be a direct reflection on you and vice versa. Be sure that the person you are introducing to your network will reflect on you positively. And when someone introduces you to someone else, be respectful regarding interactions with them.

When you network with intentionality, you will find more time on your calendar for productive work time and a little more cash in your pocket.

> **#RebelMindset: Networking is one of the fastest ways to accomplish the KNOW | LIKE | TRUST in your marketing.**

Be sure to complete the Networking on Purpose table with Places/People/Pitch sections as part of your overall marketing strategy.

Review Your RebelMindset:

- Lead generation is not the only reason to network.
- Be patient and know there are various stages and goals of networking.
- Show up consistently and be authentic.

Chapter 10 Worksheet

Network on Purpose

Lead Generation	Community	Education
Places	Places	Places
People	People	People
Pitch	Pitch	Pitch

Conclusion: Feeding Your RebelMindset

CONGRATULATIONS! You are on the way to market your business like a REBEL!

I have read many business books, yet there is one thing that I miss from the experience... being able to dive deeper into the content and ask questions of the author. Well, I am getting rid of that roadblock. Click on the QR code below or go to my website at www.rebelgirlmarketing.com and book your session to attend a virtual Q&A session with me.

Intentionality. If I were to pick one word to represent how to add a #RebelMindset to your marketing strategy, it's intentionality. Create strategies that are intentional in knowing:

- Why you need marketing in the first place
- What you sell and the emotions tied to your product/service
- Whom to sell it to and where they hang out
- What to say that starts great conversations
- How to network on purpose

Marketing Is a Mindset. As you walk through your day, remember to be cognitive of how you are interacting with others, internally and externally. Marketing is perception, so be sure you are being perceived by others the way you want to be.

Small businesses are the backbone of any community. What we need right now are stronger communities and that includes your business being here today and for years to come! The only thing that is keeping you from growing your business is your personal "Tina" that is inhibiting you from being the best version of yourself. Get rid of your limiting belief and tell your Tina to $#(@ off!

Marketing Is a Team Sport. Share what you wrote in each chapter with others in your organization, your mastermind group, your business coach, or your mentor to gain their insights on how to keep your business moving forward. As business leaders, we can get stuck in the weeds. It is always a good idea to engage others and see your business from a different perspective.

> **#RebelMindset: Marketing is simply storytelling and selling is simply telling that story to others.**

If you enjoyed this book, be sure to visit my website for information on other services I have to offer and speaking engagement topics. rebelgirlmarketing.com

Always remember, there are benefits to a #RebelMindset!

For your convenience, here are the Review Your RebelMindset takeaways for each chapter, as well as book recommendations:

Part I: Marketing Strategy

Chapter 1: The Rebel Reboot
- Marketing is what you do…branding is what people say about you.
- KNOW & LIKE is marketing…going from LIKE to TRUST is selling.

CONCLUSION: FEEDING YOUR REBELMINDSET

- Be consistent, mix your channels and use the senses and be remembered.

Chapter 2: Stop Committing Random Acts of Marketing
- Know why you need marketing.
- It's an investment, not budget.
- Marketing is a team sport; who's on your team?

Chapter 3: What Are You *Really* Selling?
- Do you sell a product, service, or both?
- Differentiators set you apart and increase brand awareness.
- Price is a matter of perceived value: quality and/or convenience.

Chapter 4: Ideal Customer vs Target Audience: Know the Difference
- Demographics: tangible characteristics.
- Psychographics: intangible characteristics.
- Channels: where does your ideal customer hang out?
  - Pick 2 channels to use and do them very, very well!

Chapter 5: Quit Sounding Like Everyone Else
- Power Pitch is less than 15 seconds, shows how you add value or tells your WHY.
- Use words that your audience will connect with.
- Practice to become professional.

Part 2: Taking Your Marketing Knowledge to the Next Level

Chapter 6: Everything Is Marketing: Yes, Everything
- Marketing is a mindset, it's in everything you do during your workday.
- Your online presence is your first impression with new customers.
- Listen to learn, not to respond.

Chapter 7: Selling – It's Easier Than You Think
- Selling is simply informing and storytelling.
- Practice active listening to hear the real needs of the customer.
- Be authentic and sell with passion and conviction.

Chapter 8: The Power of Giving
- Use B.A.N.T. to qualify leads.
- Go Fish! is not just for kids anymore.
- Keeping score is forbidden in this game.

Chapter 9: Marketing Is a Team Sport
- Build brand ambassadors.
- Make sure your team knows your story.
- Become an employer of choice.

Chapter 10: Networking on Purpose
- Lead generation is not the only reason to network.
- Be patient and know there are various stages and goals of networking.
- Show up consistently and be authentic.

Here are a few topics that need a deeper dive; topics I will be working on writing in the future:
- Sales and Marketing – two functions, one overarching goal – it's time for these two roles to start playing nice in the sandbox!
- Your Customers' Journey – is it smooth and enjoyable or full of potholes and gravel?
- The Power of Your Pitch – an experiential learning process that includes one-to-one time with me.

Books Recommendations:
- MINDSET: To learn more about the concept of mindset as it pertains to business, I recommend *The Infinite Game* by Simon Sinek
- SALES: If you would like to learn more about the art of selling, I suggest reading *Oh Sh*t I'm in Sales? The Entrepreneurs Guide to Making Sales Your BFF* by Susan Trumpler.
- NETWORKING: Joe Sweeney, the author of *Networking Is a Contact Sport.* If you would like to dive deeper into learning about networking, I suggest Joe's book as well as *Radical Relevance* by Bill Cates. Both books go into how to strategically use networking in your marketing efforts.

About the Author

Meet the REBEL of Rebel Girl Marketing. As the Founder, Speaker, and Chief Storyteller of Rebel Girl Marketing, Lisa developed her proprietary RebelMindset approach after more than twenty-five years as a successful marketing executive and leading sales professional. Her mission: to help businesses stay in business by utilizing focused, uncompromising marketing strategies. Lisa cuts through the noise and breaks marketing down to what makes sense for her customers, creating strategies that are simple, relatable to their target audiences, and which result in double-digit sales growth year after year.

What sets Lisa apart in the world of marketing is her ability to help professionals make a great first impression by teaching them to create inspirational, attention-getting Power Pitches. After talking with Lisa, you will find out that there are benefits to a RebelMindset!

When Lisa is not working, she is spending time with her two children and husband of 28 years. Her passion for inspiration is found in her cooking, paddle boarding in Lake Country, or enjoying long hikes through the numerous trails in southeast Wisconsin.